THE OMNIPRESENT I AM

I AM

Volume One

Writings by the Author

The Ultimate

Prayers and Excerpts from The Word

Success Is Normal, Just Be Yourself,
   Your Eternal Identity

Fulfillment of Purpose, Volume One

Fulfillment of Purpose, Volume Two

You Are the Splendor

Gems & Poems of The Ultimate

The Gospel According to Thomas

Three Essential Steps

The Omnipresent I AM, Volume One

The Omnipresent I AM, Evidenced, Volume Two

The Ultimate Awareness, an Eternal Constant,
   Volume One

The Ultimate Awareness, an Eternal Constant,
   Volume Two

These and other books available through:
Mystics of the World
Eliot, Maine
www.mysticsoftheworld.com

THE OMNIPRESENT I AM

Volume One

Marie S. Watts

The Omnipresent I AM
Volume One
by Marie S. Watts

Mystics of the World First Edition 2015 1966
Published by Mystics of the World
ISBN-13: 978-0692565476
ISBN-10: 0692565477

For information contact:
Mystics of the World
Eliot, Maine
www.mysticsoftheworld.com

Photography by © Dr. Joel Murphy 2015
www.DrJMphotography.zenfolio.com
Printed by CreateSpace
Available from Mystics of the World and Amazon.com

Contents

Note to the Student

Dear One,

In your study and contemplation of volumes one and two of these classnotes, you will discover that the entire basis for all that is revealed herein is stated in the first four chapters of this book. Actually, the basic Truths revealed in these chapters are a thorough preparation for the revelations that you will experience as you continue in your study of these books. Therefore, I feel impelled to recommend that you read, *Chap 1,2,3,4 then chap 1* and then re-read, from page one of this book through page ten. If you will follow this procedure before continuing on into the text of this classwork, you will experience glorious revelations, and these revelations will continue to be your experience. Furthermore, you will clearly perceive that all that is revealed is Self-revealed. *It is the I AM that you are, revealing Itself as Itself.*

I have no words with which to tell you the boundless, surging, flowing Love and Joy I experience in presenting these revelations just as they have been revealed.

Love Eternal and Immeasurable,
Marie S. Watts

Introduction

This is the first of two volumes of classwork, which represents the most glorious and enlightened class we have ever experienced. Due to your numerous requests that this classwork be available, we lovingly present these revelations, in order that you may have an opportunity to study and contemplate them as devotedly as you will.

The purpose of these writings is that ~~the student~~ *you* may completely transcend all illusory sense of a selfhood or an existence separate from or other than the infinite, indivisible, omniactive Omnipresence. Virtually every difficulty we ever seem to experience, no matter what may be its name or its nature, is due to the apparent inability to perceive our universal, inseparable Oneness. To truly perceive is to *be* that which is perceived. Aware of *being* that which we perceive, *we are the evidence* of our conscious awareness of this Truth.

Often we hear someone speak of being one *with* God. In this very statement, there is duality, or twoness. To be one *with* God would mean that the identity had a life, mind, consciousness, that was independent as itself yet that a union *between* God and this identity could be accomplished or experienced.

Our basic premise is *God is All*. This being true, then *All is God*. God is the *only* Presence; the *only*

8

Presence is God. God is the only One present; the only One present is God. God is Omniaction, the only Activity; Omniaction — the only Activity — is God in action. God is the only Substance; the only Substance is God. God is the only Form; the only Form is God — and there is no Substance in Form that is not God. God is the only Substance in action; the only Substance in action is God acting.

Many students of the Absolute have recognized the Truth as It is expressed in these words. Furthermore, these students have inherently felt that these words of Truth were irrefutable. Yet the full and complete realization has seemed to elude them — that the omnipresent Omniaction which is God, and God in action, is all there is of their Body and Being. Why is this true? It is true because they have not yet completely perceived just how it is, and why it is, that it is utterly impossible for them to have or to be anything or anyone apart from, or other than, God. The perception of this tremendous fact requires full knowledge.

It has been said that knowledge is power, and this is true. But the knowledge that is a power is not *acquired* knowledge. It is not something that is learned. True knowledge must always be *revealed*, and the revelation must be experienced within and *as* the Consciousness of the Identity himself or herself. All revelation is Self-revelation. No revelation can be taught. No revelation can be imparted. No revelation can be learned. All revelation is experienced as

9

illumined, or enlightened, Consciousness reveals Itself to *be* the Allness, the Isness, the Nowness, and the Hereness of God—and God *being* just what God is. Thus, the Identity is aware of *being* and, consequently, of being just what God is and nothing else.

The Truths revealed in these volumes of classwork are truly revelation. Most important is the fact that students who attended these class sessions clearly perceived that these revelations were being experienced within and as their own Consciousness. Many wonderful things took place during these sessions, and some of these glorious experiences would be, in world terminology, called miracles.

It is our firm conviction that those who read, study, and contemplate the absolute, irrefutable Truths herein revealed will experience ever greater and more illumined Self-revelations. And we know that the knowledge thus perceived will be the Presence of the Power and the Power of the Presence as the experience of the reader. Thus, this classwork is lovingly dedicated to You who read and who know that you *are* every Truth herein revealed.

Boundless Light and Love,
Marie S. Watts

or infinitely, present. Because the word *Omni* means All, these Truths mean that there is nothing present here and now that is not eternally, infinitely, constantly present. *All* means *All*, and nothing besides or other than *All*, or Omnipresence, exists.

It goes without saying that there is no vacuum or vacancy in Omnipresence. A vacuum would mean an absence of *anything*. This is impossible because Omnipresence is present. Indeed, Omnipresence is present everywhere because it is *the* Everywhere. But this is not all: Omnipresence is *equally* present everywhere. Being a Universal Constant, It is present constantly; thus, It is never absent. There is not an instant in eternity when Omnipresence is not present equally everywhere. You see, there is no vacuum in Eternity any more than there is a vacuum in Infinity. Actually, eternity and infinity are identical, for there is neither time nor space. (Incidentally, the space physicists know this to be true.)

Of course, I realize that to speak in this way at the very beginning of this class experience may be somewhat shocking. You will read many statements that at first are startling in this book. But bear with us, and you will perceive how It is, and why it is, that each one of these statements is true. You will also discover why it is impossible for these statements of Absolute Truth not to be true.

If we were to base our concept of Existence upon the world of appearance, it would be ridiculous to make these statements or to believe them. But the world is not what it appears to be. Any one of the leading physicists will tell you that this world, its Substance and Activity, is not the way it appears to be.

Let us now return to the wonderful word *Omnipresence*. Let us perceive, at least to some extent, what constitutes Omnipresence. One aspect of Omnipresence is Consciousness. In order to know that we exist, we have to be conscious. Thus, we know that Consciousness is present. Therefore, Consciousness is omnipresent. Indeed, Consciousness is Omnipresence Itself.

We have to be alive in order to be conscious. Hence, Life exists. It is present. Life *is* Omnipresence. Omnipresent Consciousness is Omnipresence. Therefore, we perceive that omnipresent, conscious Life is Omnipresence. Also, omnipresent, *living* Consciousness is Omnipresence.

In our consideration of any Truth, our approach is first from the standpoint of the Universe. Let us realize that there is a distinction — but not a separation — between the Universe and our Earth planet. When we speak of the Universe, we mean Infinity, or the boundless Completeness that *is* the Universe. When we speak of the world, we are speaking of our immediate solar system, including our Earth planet.

It is obvious that this is an *intelligent* Universe. There is intelligent activity constantly present in and as this Universe. It requires Intelligence, or Mind, to maintain and sustain such perfect order and control as that which is apparent as the Universe, and this perfect order and control is universal, it is constant, and it is eternal. It is always present, and it is everywhere present. Thus, Mind—Intelligence—is omnipresent, meaning that Mind is Omnipresence. Living, conscious Mind is Omnipresence. Intelligent, conscious Life is Omnipresence. Conscious, intelligent Life is Omnipresence.

Now we have arrived at the aspect of Omnipresence which is perhaps the most important of all—namely *Love*. Love is a living Presence. Love is Life. Love is a *conscious* Presence. Love is Consciousness. Love is an intelligent Presence. Love is Mind.

What is the basis for the foregoing statements? Oneness is the basis for these statements, and Love is the inseparable Oneness of Consciousness, Life, Mind. Love is the indivisible Oneness of our infinite Entirety. This is why this Universe functions so perfectly and so harmoniously. The inseparable Oneness of all Existence is Love, and this Love is Omnipresent. It is indeed Omnipresence.

We will now discuss the word *Omniaction*. We know that this is an active Universe. Activity is universally present; It is constantly present and It is eternally present. It is clear that Activity is omnipresent. Thus, Activity is Omnipresence. Life Itself is Activity. Without Activity there could be no Life. But without Life there could be no Activity either. We know that Life is everywhere. We know that Life is constant, without an interruption, and that Life is eternal. Indeed, Life is universal, and It is equally present eternally and infinitely. There are no vacuums in Life. Life is ever and everlastingly active. It is *everywhere* active. Life is *all* that is active. Therefore, Life is Omniaction and Omniaction is Life. But Life, Consciousness, Mind, Love are One. They are inseparably One. Hence, we can see that Consciousness, Mind, Life, Love are omniactive. Thus, Omniaction is conscious, living, intelligent Love.

It is obvious that Omniaction is Mind in action because the stars, the planets, the Earth planet, and the galaxies function, or act, so perfectly. The perfect Activity that governs Itself as this Universe is Mind in action. It is Consciousness in action. It is Love in action. In fact, It is living, conscious, loving Mind — Intelligence — in action. And most important of all is the fact that this perfect Mind in action is all the Activity there is, has ever been, or can ever be. It is eternal, constant, without an interruption or a vacuum. It is equally present everywhere, eternally and constantly. *We* are conscious Activity; hence, this Activity, or Omniaction, is living, intelligent, loving Consciousness. All that is conscious is Consciousness. Thus, Consciousness is omniactive and It is Omniaction.

Now we have considered the four words that symbolize the omniactive Omnipresence that was mentioned in the title of this class. But there is more to this title than just these four symbolic words. I AM is also included in the title. And none of this Truth would fulfill any purpose in and *as* your experience if you — your Self — were not this Truth. It is never enough just to know that some Truth is true. To know the Truth *about* something or someone is incomplete knowledge, if such could be.

Furthermore, this incomplete knowing is duality. It is assuming that there is a Truth *and* an Identity for it to be true about. Hence, it seems that Truth is separate from the Identity. Jesus knew — and knows — better than this. He said, "I am the Truth," and he knew exactly what he meant. You *are* the Truth. *You* are the omnipresent, omniactive, omnipotent, living, conscious, loving Mind that is ever present. Yes, You are this Mind that is *All that is present*. And is this not being Omnipresence? Indeed so!

You can say:

> I am alive, and Life is the only thing that is alive. Thus, I am Life *being* alive. I am conscious, and there is nothing conscious but Consciousness. Hence, I am Consciousness *being* conscious. I am living Consciousness, or Consciousness alive. There is nothing intelligent but Mind or Intelligence. I am intelligent. Hence, I am Mind *being* intelligent. I am living, conscious Mind. I am conscious, living Mind. I am intelligent, conscious Life. I am intelligent, living Consciousness.

> Nothing loves but Love. I love. I am conscious, living, loving Mind. I am intelligent, loving, conscious Life. I am conscious, intelligent, living Love. I am active. The Life I am is Activity. I am Life, thus I *am* Activity. I am all Life, all Mind, all Consciousness, all Love.

> This Allness that I am is the Entirety of the *I* that I am. And the Entirety — the sum total — of all

that I am in action is Omniaction. Therefore, I am Omniaction. I am living, conscious, loving Mind in action. This is why I am conscious, intelligent Activity, and this is why I am conscious, loving, harmonious Activity.

I know that I exist right here and right now. In order to know that I exist here and now, *I must be present right here and now.* There is nothing present but Omnipresence. I am present; thus, I am Omnipresence. I am all Presence. I am the Infinite Presence. I am the eternal, beginningless, endless Presence. I am the constant, uninterrupted Presence. I am the Presence of the sum total of all Truth, or all that is true. I am the Presence of eternal, constant, conscious Life. I am the Presence of eternal, living Consciousness. I am the Presence of uninterrupted, constant Perfection. I am the Presence of changeless, living, constant, eternal Love.

Only that which is present has, or is, Power. Omnipresence is omnipotent, for Omnipresence is Omnipotence, The Presence I am is the Power I am. The Power I am is the Presence I am. I am the omnipotent Omni-presence. I am the omnipresent Omnipotence.

What is the Power that I am? The Omnipotence that I am is the Power of knowing what I am and of being what I know my Self to be. I am not power over anything or anyone. I am solely the Power of knowing and of being. Knowing and being are One, and I am that One. To know is to *be* what I know. To *be* is to know what I am. Furthermore, to know is to *be* All that I know. And to *be* is to know All that I am. Thus, I am omnipresent Omnipotence, and I am omnipotent Omnipresence.

Beloved, does the foregoing I AM revelation seem too mystical or too ephemeral for you? Does it sound too Absolute to be practical? Don't be deceived. What we have perceived just now is the very basis for all joyous, perfect, peaceful, successful living. No matter what Truth you may realize, you can be assured that It is eternally established in these revelations. And above all, if there were such a thing as "treatment," this would be the most complete treatment one could possibly experience.

I know that the foregoing statements of Truth will bear much study and contemplation. I also know that the more you study and contemplate these revealed Truths, the greater will be your realization and your evidence of joy, peace, Perfection, Completeness, and complete success in and as every aspect of your daily affairs.

You see, because we are to go so far in our perception of this Truth during our class experience, it is necessary to experience the fundamental or basic Truths very early in this exceedingly Absolute and enlightening revelation of Absolute Truth. It may be compared to the building of a house. Your structure can only be as great, as expansive, and as substantial as is its foundation.

There is another tremendously important aspect of the value in first perceiving the Truth from the standpoint of the omnipotent Omnipresence: in this perception, we are instantaneously free from any personal sense. There can be—and is—no little separate "I" in the perception of these basic Truths.

For instance, what little so-called person could say, "I am omnipotent Omnipresence"? Wouldn't that be the very height or depth of self-deception? In fact, it would be ridiculous. In beginning our glorious class experience in this basic, universal way, there can be no assumptive, little, limited "I" that seems to block and to conceal the infinite, eternal, constant *I* that I am.

Of course, you realize that this is but another way of approaching all Truth from the Universal standpoint. It is saying, "Your Consciousness is your Universe." But it is also saying, "Your Universe is your Consciousness." It is really more simple and direct to say:

> I, the Universal *I* that I am, is the specific I
> that I am. The specific I that I am is the Universal
> *I* that I am.

Chapter II

Substance

The two primary Existents we must clearly perceive are Substance and Activity. All Existence is Substance, and all Activity is Substance in action. Substance *is* Omnipresence, and Substance in action is Omniaction. In order that there be Activity, there must be something to act. There is — and this Something that acts is Substance.

Let us not be deceived by the word *Substance*. Few there are who understand the meaning of this word. If, to you, it has a connotation of solidity, density, or of something material, by all means reject the word and substitute the word *Essence*. Once you really know what Substance is, it won't make any difference what word you accept as a symbol for Substance. So let us, right here and now, discover just what we mean when we use the word *Substance*.

Let us examine some definitions of this word *Substance* as found in Webster's Dictionary. His first definition is:

> That which underlies all outward mani-festation; reality itself; the abiding part of any existence, in distinction to that which is accidental to it.; the permanent and identical in any process of change; the real essence or nature of a thing.

Well, these definitions do not sound as though Substance were matter. That which is called "matter" is only the so-called "outward manifestation" or "false appearance" of the Identity Itself. Actually, until we see with the eye that is single, the so-called outward manifestation, or appearance, of anything only seems to conceal the genuine and *only* Substance, or Essence, of the Substance in form that really exists. So we can see that the *appearance* of the Substance in form is not at all the Substance that *is*. Rather, it is the distorted and misleading way the Substance in form appears to be but is not.

Often we have pointed out the fact that the physicists have proven that something seems to happen between the eye that is supposed to see an object and the object itself. They frankly state that the eye does not see Substance as It is. If they have discovered and accepted, from their materialistic basis, this much that is true, surely we should be able to accept and have faith in this Absolute Truth.

Anything that seems to begin and to end is not Substance. Anything that appears to be solid, or blocked off in so-called space, is not Substance. Anything that appears to be separate from all that supposedly surrounds it is not Substance. Anything that seems to be dark or dense is not Substance. All of these deceptive appearances are sheer illusion, without an iota of Reality in them. Certain it is that an illusion is not Substance.

Substance, by Its very Nature, is perfect. There is no such thing as imperfect Substance. Any appearance of imperfection is simply an appearance and nothing else. Substance is everywhere. It is infinite. It is everywhere equally and everywhere the same. Now they have discovered that the cells of the tree trunk are the same kind of cells that are supposed to be body cells. They are getting closer to the truth, anyway. But we know the true Nature of that which is called cells, and this true Nature is the genuine and *only* Substance.

Now, we have discussed quite thoroughly what Substance is not. Let us, therefore, discuss what Substance *is*. For years, we have heard that Spirit is Substance. We have read much about spiritual Substance. But the meaning of the word *Spirit* has been little comprehended. Let us symbolize this Substance by the use of words that clarify and define the Absolute Nature of Substance.

We have said that Substance is everywhere, or omnipresent. We have also said that Substance is eternal, constant, and changeless. What could be infinite, eternal, and omnipresent other than Omnipresence Itself? We have already perceived the Nature of Omnipresence. We know that Omnipresence is perfect, eternal, infinite Life, Consciousness, Mind, Love. So here is our answer: perfect, eternal, universal Life, Consciousness, Mind, Love are the Substance we have called Spirit, or spiritual Substance.

This entire boundless Universe is Substance. It is living Substance. This Universe is alive. It is a living, intelligent Substance. Of course It would have to be a living, intelligent Substance because It *is* Life and It *is* Mind. It is obvious that this Universe is a living Substance, for there is constant activity everywhere in and as this Universe. The very air itself is constantly alive, and Activity is Life. We can clearly perceive that this is an intelligent Universe by the intelligent, orderly, balanced, perfectly controlled way in which this universal Activity functions. Let us make no mistake about it—it takes Mind, or Intelligence, to maintain and sustain the Activity of the Universal Substance in such a perfect, orderly, harmonious, controlled manner.

Now we realize that Substance is alive and that Substance is intelligent. We know that living Intelligence is inseparable from Consciousness. (By the way, the word *Consciousness* is a wonderful synonym for Substance.) Consciousness is Awareness. It comprises the Universe—All Substance—aware of being what It *is* and aware of being *All that It is*.

Just let us consider this magnificent fact for a moment: Consciousness is Omnipresence. It is present equally everywhere, infinitely and eternally. Consciousness is constant, without an interruption and without a vacuum. Do you see what this means? It means that there is not so much as one infinitesimal so-called atom, cell, etc., that does not consist of Consciousness aware of being what It is.

What is Consciousness aware of being? It is aware of being eternal, perfect, intelligent, loving Life. It is eternally aware of being alive. It is wonderful to realize that this Consciousness that is aware of being eternally and constantly alive is Substance.

It is *your* Substance. It is the Substance that comprises this Body right here, now, eternally. And this, Beloved, is *your* Substance, aware of *being* what It is.

Chapter III

Omniscience

You know that the word *Omniscience* means all knowledge. What is it that has, or *is*, all knowledge? Infinite Mind, eternal Mind, omnipresent Mind, constant Mind, is all knowledge. This Mind that is all knowledge is Substance. You are intelligent, and there is nothing intelligent but Intelligence, or Mind. You are aware of having or being Substance. The Intelligence, Mind, that you are is the Substance you are. The Mind that you are does not have to wait in order to have or to be any knowledge. The only Mind there is, is the all-knowing Mind. All-knowing means all knowledge. And this, Beloved, is Omniscience. Being Mind Itself, you are the complete Intelligence that is all knowledge. Thus, *you* are Omniscience.

So often it seems that we should know some fact and yet this knowledge eludes us. For instance, many of us have felt, in periods of stress or seeming problems, that there just had to be some specific Truth that would reveal the perfect evidence that seemed to be so necessary. We have felt that if we could only know this one specific Truth, Perfection would be revealed and evidenced. Please be assured that any Truth necessary for you to know, you can—

and do—know every moment. This is true because you *are* all knowledge, or Omniscience.

Chapter IV

Consciousness

You may wonder just how it is possible for you to be aware of any Truth at any moment. Ah, here we have arrived at the word *Consciousness*. It is possible, Beloved, because you are conscious—and only Consciousness is conscious. Consciousness is the instantaneity of all knowledge. There is never a so-called past or future in—or as—Consciousness. Actually, Consciousness is the here and the now of all knowledge, or Omniscience. You are never conscious of being yesterday or tomorrow. You are only conscious of being *now*.

Of course, it may seem that you are remembering something that was experienced in an illusory past. Or it may appear that you intuitively sense something that is going to take place in an illusory future. But there is neither a past, nor is there a future. Even a so-called memory of the past, at the moment of remembrance, is present right now in and as Consciousness.

In like manner, something that you are positive will transpire in an illusory future has to be present as your Consciousness this moment, else it would never occur to you. Thus, you can perceive that the so-called past is *now* and the so-called future is *now*.

This completely obliterates the necessity for any memory or any seeming necessity to remember something called a past event. But this is also why any Truth you ever have known or that you ever will know is present as the knowledge that you *are*, right now.

Consciousness does not wait to be aware. It is constantly, consciously aware of being. Consciousness is Mind, even as Mind is Consciousness. Consciousness, Mind, is Substance. Conscious All-knowledge, or Omniscience, is Substance. The conscious, omniscient Mind that you are is the *only* Substance that you have, or *are*, here, now, eternally.

This Substance in Form called the Body does not have to wait in order to know that It is perfect, conscious Mind right now. Neither does It need to experience delay in *being* the evidence of the constant, eternal Perfection that It eternally is. Your Consciousness, awareness, that you exist right here and now is your instant and constant awareness of anything you wish to know or to be, right here and now.

This is the beautiful thing about Consciousness. It is *instant*. You, this instant, are conscious that you exist. You, this instant, are not conscious that you exist yesterday or tomorrow. You are only conscious of being *now*. Consciousness is not an awareness of being yesterday or tomorrow. Consciousness is only an awareness of being *now*.

We have stated that you are Omniscience, or all knowledge. The awareness of being what you are

29

this instant is the Intelligence that is Omniscience, and this omniscient Consciousness is your Substance in Form, or the Body that you *are*. From this you can perceive why the Perfection that you may be seeking is here, now. It is instantaneous. It is simultaneous with your awareness that you exist. It has to be this way, Beloved, because the omniscient Consciousness you are *is* the Body you are, and the Body you are *is* the conscious Omniscience you are. Now, how can there be a delay in the evidence of the Perfection that you consciously are this instant? There cannot be, and there is not one second of postponement of the evidence of your conscious Perfection.

Someone has said, "I think, therefore I am." Well, so-called thinking is no guarantee that you exist. But Consciousness *is* Existence. You will note that in the Ultimate we do not speak of thinking. Neither do we speak of human memory. Thinking implies time, and there is no time. Memory also implies time, which does not exist. Truth alone exists. Time is not true; thus, it is not Truth. Here, in the Ultimate, all is *now*.

Why is this true? It is true because right now we are conscious, and Consciousness is complete. Consciousness is complete, infinite, eternal Omnipresence. Consciousness is Omniscience, the all-knowing Mind. All knowledge is here and now. We do not have to wait in order to know anything. Consciousness never waits to become conscious. Omniscience does not wait to become all knowledge.

We have seemed to bind ourselves unmercifully. We have apparently erected our own seeming prison walls, and we have made the building stones of our apparent prison out of ages of accumulated false knowledge. These fictitious, illusory prison walls are only the misconceptions of a kind of mind — or man — that does not even exist, and these misconceptions instantly dissolve into the nothingness they are — and have always been — the very moment we are aware of being complete, *conscious*, omniscient Mind. Yes, the awareness of being all knowledge means the instantaneous evidence of our awareness. And this, Beloved, is the *only* Substance you have or that you are.

There is much more to be revealed pertaining to this word *knowledge*, and we will very soon return to further exploration of this wonderful aspect of Completeness. But now let us just realize that we *are* the universal, constant, eternal, conscious Mind that is all Substance. We can perceive that the I AM that *you are* is the constant presence of complete knowledge of all that you are. This constant, conscious, living Mind is never static. Always It is active, and the activity of the universal Substance that you are is Omniaction. What is the universal Substance that you are? Mind, Consciousness, Life, Love comprise the infinite, complete, boundless Substance that you are. And this glorious Substance in action is Omniaction. So you can see that *you are Omniaction*.

Now we have discussed the basis of all the Truth that is to be revealed during the morning class experience. We have prepared the foundation, in a manner of speaking, and we are ready for the magnificent revelations that are the complete structure. This complete structure consists solely of the universal, living, loving, conscious Mind that is all Substance, and this Mind is omnipotent, omniactive Omnipresence.

Reread from P 11

Chapter V

Knowledge Is Power

You might wonder just what all of this Truth pertaining to the Universe has to do with your living experience right here. Actually, it has *everything* to do with your entire daily experience right here and now. It enables you to live freely, joyously, and without effort. It takes all the strain and struggle out of your daily life. It enables you to live successfully, and you find that this success is omniactive in and *as* every activity of your daily experience. Furthermore, you discover that the Substance in Form called your Body is perfect and is functioning, acting, perfectly. Always be aware of the fact that any Truth you perceive is true as the Substance and Activity of your Body is also true as your daily affairs.

Now, why is our knowledge of being this Truth so powerful in and as our Body and our daily experience? It is powerful because *knowledge is power*. Yes, knowledge is power. But this statement must be clarified. We must understand what kind of knowledge we are speaking about. The knowledge that is power is not *acquired* knowledge. It has nothing to do with knowledge that is attained through educational methods, in which instructors are supposed to impart or to add knowledge to students.

This is no criticism of schools, colleges, or universities. I know that they fulfill a definite purpose just now. Nonetheless, genuine knowledge cannot be taught, nor can it be acquired. It simply *is*, because the *only* Mind in existence is Omniscience, or all knowledge. And because this complete Omniscience is the Consciousness of every Identity, the omniscient Mind that is every Identity is complete Knowledge. The only way to be aware of knowledge is to know and to know completely, and the only way to know completely is to know from the universal standpoint. The only way to know what you are—and all that you are—is to know what comprises this entire Universe.

You see, you are not a separate little particle of something existing and functioning all alone here. You are not always struggling to become joyous, free, healthy, successful, etc. Neither are you striving to free your Self from limitations. There simply is no circumference around you that confines you to a little, limited life or to a small area. The Consciousness you are is as boundless as is the Universe, for the Consciousness you are *is* the boundless Universe Itself. As we have so often stated, "There is nowhere that the Universe leaves off and you begin. Neither is there a line of demarcation where you leave off and the Universe begins." It is all one indivisible, infinite One, and *You* are that *One*. I am that *One*. Everyone is that inseparable, constant, eternal *One*.

It is the universal, conscious, omniscient Mind that you are aware of being that is *power*. This knowledge is power, but it is not knowledge that can be taught. It cannot be acquired or attained. Already it is present *as* the conscious Mind that you are. So this knowledge must be revealed within and *as* the very Consciousness that *you* are. This is the kind of knowledge that is power. In fact, it is omnipotent Intelligence Itself. This complete, Self-revealed knowledge is indeed power. But it is not power over anyone or anything. It is simply the power of knowing what you are and of *being* what you know. Furthermore, it is the power of evidencing what you know and know your Self to be.

In a way, our discoveries from the Ultimate standpoint may be compared to the discoveries of Dr. Einstein. You will recall that his approach was also from the universal standpoint. We do not approach this Truth from the somewhat limited viewpoint of metaphysics. As a matter of fact, metaphysics has been defined as just one step beyond physics, and this is true. But the same seeming limitations that are encountered in the study of physics are also present in the study of metaphysics. In physics, we have the so-called law of cause and effect, and we find this same spurious belief in virtually all of the teachings of metaphysics. There are various other points of similarity between physics and metaphysics, but we shall not probe into these similarities just now. Our point is that we, even as Dr. Einstein, perceive Truth from the universal standpoint.

Before Dr. Einstein's investigations, the physicists were primarily concerned with exploring the most infinitesimal particles of so-called matter they could discover. In this way, they hoped to discover the nature of all Substance. Of course, they are still investigating ever smaller particles of what they call matter. Yet they are now aware of the fact that the Substance of the Universe is also the Substance of every so-called atom and item that comprises this Infinity. Still, their exploration is mainly from the atom to the Universe.

Dr. Einstein, even as we, began his explorations from the standpoint of the Universe Itself. Inherently he knew that whatever was the Nature of the Universe was also the Nature of the infinitesimal Substance in Form that could ever be discovered. Of course, it is now claimed by some physicists that some of Dr. Einstein's theories are wrong. And perhaps this is true. Any investigation of the Nature of Substance from the standpoint of so-called matter must, of necessity, be faulty and incomplete. This is true because matter does not exist.

It is now frankly admitted by many physicists that matter, as such, does not exist. They even say that matter is nothing but illusion. But it has taken the discoveries of Dr. Einstein, from the universal standpoint, to bring about this realization on the part of contemporary physicists.

Of course, our seeming search, as well as the search by metaphysicians, has been for Truth, or for that which is true. However, metaphysics, even as the physicists prior to Dr. Einstein, confined its search to the so-called separate particle of the All, called the individual.

There are students of metaphysics who attempt to concentrate the entire mind at the most infinitesimal point possible. Then they attempt to expand this mind from this point *to* the Universe. But of course, this so-called method of meditation is limited. It begins by limiting the attention to the confines of an infinitesimal point. Naturally, its viewpoint must be, and is, subject to these self-imposed limitations.

We, however, even as Dr. Einstein, begin all of our contemplation from the standpoint of the Universal All Itself. Thus, we are unlimited in our revelations. We are aware of the fact that whatever the Universe is, *That* are we. We know that this Universe is one inseparable All, or Omnipresence. And we realize that in order to exist, or *to be present*, we have to exist *as* just what this Universe is and nothing else.

Of course, once we have perceived the infinite, boundless Nature of the Universe and that *we are that boundless Infinity and That alone*, we can then be specific. By this I mean that we can—and do—then perceive the fact that the specific Identity right here and now is exactly the same Substance and Activity that comprises the one indivisible, universal All. And of course, we realize that the one boundless, universal All is our infinite, conscious, living Identity.

Nonetheless, it is knowledge of being both the universal Identity and the specific Identity that enables us to live so freely, so harmoniously, so perfectly, and so joyously. But above all, never do we make the mistake of believing that the specific Identity is separate from or other than the universal Identity. Actually, as we shall presently see, the universal Identity *is* the specific Identity, even as the specific Identity *is* the universal Identity.

It is this knowledge that enables us to realize and manifest an unlimited abundance of all that is good and right. This means that we perceive and evidence an abundance of health, Love, wealth— even though it be called money. And above all, we are aware of *being* a constantly abundant, effortless fulfillment of purpose. All of this glorious experience takes place through our knowledge of the Nature of our universal Identity and through the knowledge that whatever the universal Identity is, our specific Identity is, right here and now.

Yes, knowledge is power. By this statement, we do not mean knowledge of a fictitious world of appearance. After all, this world of appearance is sheer illusion, even as the physicists now realize. This apparent world does appear to be matter, and matter is illusion. Thus, matter is not Substance. An illusion is not Substance. An illusion is not active. In order that there be activity, there must be something to act, and this Something has to be Substance. It is impossible for an illusion to be activity because it has—or is—not Substance. Therefore, there is neither illusory activity, nor is there illusory substance, called matter, to act.

Sometimes it does seem difficult to realize that Substance is not matter and matter is not Substance. Often we hear someone ask, "What is the difference between Substance and matter?" Well, that which appears to be matter is the way the genuine and *only* Substance appears—but is not—when we are not actually seeing the Substance that is right before us. What is this Substance that we misinterpret as matter? It is Life, Mind, Consciousness, Love, in Form. And of course, all of this Substance is Light. All Substance is Light. It is knowledge that enables us to actually see Substance *as It is*. And what a beautiful and glorious Life we experience being when we do actually *see* that which is here to see.

Yes, again we must say, "Knowledge is power." But there can be no knowledge of illusion because illusion does not exist. It is impossible to have or to be knowledge of "nothing." Can one really know what constitutes an illusion? Of course not. One could temporarily be misled or mistaken about an illusion, but it is impossible to *know* an illusion. In this same way it is impossible for anyone to actually know a lie. It can seem to deceive us for a moment. We can mistake a lie for that which is true, temporarily. But we simply cannot *know* a lie. It is nothing, and being nothing, it cannot be known. Only that which actually exists can be known, and that which exists is true. If there were no Truth, however, there could be no lie *about* the Truth.

The knowledge that is power is true knowledge, or knowledge of that which is true — Truth. Furthermore, this knowledge must be Self-revealed. This Self-revelation not only reveals all Truth — all that is genuine — but it also reveals that the Identity himself or herself *is* the Truth that is revealed. And this fact, Beloved, is only revealed through the realization that the revelator and the revelation are *One* and the same. Illumined Consciousness always reveals that the Identity really *is* all knowledge. It also reveals that the knowledge and the Knower are *One*.

Oh, there is Power in and as this knowledge. You see, boundless, universal Mind, aware of being Omniscience, or all knowledge, has, and *is*, the total Power that is this Universe. And of course, this is the power that is God, or Omnipotence — Mind Itself. Why is this true? It is true because this "knowing" is omnipotent, universal Mind, knowing totally and completely what It is and also knowing completely *All that It is.* It is conscious, *living* Mind, aware of being. What is this all-knowing, omnipotent, living Mind? You are.

> You are the All-knowing Mind. You are the total Omniscience that is Omnipotence Itself.

Let us see how the foregoing can be true. To know what you are means to *be* what you know. Because you are all knowledge, you do know what you are. Thus, you are the very evidence of that which you know. This is true because the all-knowing Mind that you are is your Substance. In fact, this omniscient Mind is the entirety of your Substance. This Mind that you are, actively engaged in effortless knowing, is the entirety of your effortless, but purposeful and successful, activity.

Of course, this does not mean that you are to know some Truth *about* someone or something or even *about* your Self. This would be only partial knowing. It is metaphysics and it is duality. To know, and to *know* that you know, means that you are conscious of *being* every Truth that you know. But let us be complete in this knowing. Let us realize that every Truth you are knowing *is* You. *You are the Truth*, but for complete realization and manifestation, it is necessary to perceive that every Truth you know *is you*. Truth is God. God is Truth. You are the Truth that is God. But God is also the Truth that is all there is of you. This realization would not be complete if you were not aware of the fact that the Truth you know is all there is of you, even as you are every Truth you know.

It is in this complete "knowing" that the words are so important. When you say, "I am that I AM, it is well to complete the statement by also saying, "That I AM is the *I* that I am." Herein is the completeness. Herein is the Inseparableness that is Love Itself. In this way, we have completely obliterated all false sense of being separate from or other than the Truth

41

we know. We have transcended duality, and we "stand upon the Mount" of the one infinite I AM as the specific I am. It is the specific I AM aware of being the infinite I AM. And it is the infinite I AM aware of being the specific I AM. Indeed, this knowledge is power.

Chapter VI

Knowledge, Wisdom, Understanding

Frequently I am amazed, even awed, by the Absolute Truths that are revealed in some sections of our Bible. However, if you are to recognize it for what it really means — and *is* — it is necessary to know the Absolute Truth when you read it. If every student of the Bible really knew the Absolute Truth, there would be an entirely different interpretation of many passages of the Bible. It takes the Mind that is the Absolute Truth to recognize this Truth, whenever and wherever It is revealed. Let us investigate some statements from Proverbs that will elucidate the Truths we have been, and are, perceiving.

> Happy is the man that findeth wisdom, and the man that getteth understanding ... She is more precious than rubies: and all the things thou canst desire are not to be compared unto her. Length of days is in her right hand; and in her left hand riches and honor. Her ways are ways of pleasantness, and all her paths are peace. She is a tree of life to them that lay hold upon her: and happy is every one that retaineth her" (Prov. 3: 13, 15–18).

Isn't this exactly what we have been saying? You will note that here in the third chapter of Proverbs, wisdom and understanding—just two aspects of Being—are said to be essential for happiness, abundance, health, peace, etc. But later on in Proverbs, we find another word that is considered to be of the greatest importance. This word is *knowledge*. And thus, that which is necessary for a fully joyous, free, and abundant Life is completely stated. In Proverbs 24:3-4, we read:

> Through wisdom is an house builded; and by understanding it is established: And by knowledge shall the chambers be filled with all precious and pleasant riches.

We have frequently mentioned that the figure 3 often symbolizes completeness. Here is revealed the three essentials for Absolute Completeness: wisdom, understanding, and knowledge.

Haven't we been seeking and finding wisdom throughout the years? Yes, and right here is where metaphysics did fulfill a wonderful purpose. This is why we do not criticize any metaphysical approach; however, let us continue. Haven't we read and reread countless books of Truth? Haven't we studied and contemplated the Truths we have studied? Haven't many of us been conscientious metaphysicians? And ZTruth we perceived during this study?

We did not discard one single Truth that we discovered during our study of metaphysics. We have, however, now transcended the dualistic aspects of these metaphysical teachings, and we have arrived at the understanding that God *is* All, All *is* God. But this understanding at which we have arrived means that we now perceive all Truth from the universal standpoint. We truly do understand how it is and why it is that all Existence is God, the boundless, infinite, conscious being that you are and that I am and that everyone is.

Now we have arrived at the third word, the word that signifies completeness. This word is *knowledge*. It matters not how much Truth we have learned or how well we understand this Truth; it takes a certain knowledge if we are to completely transcend *all* duality, and this certain knowledge is our perception that *we are every Truth we believe, know, or understand.*

This, Beloved, is the I AM knowledge. When we are aware of being every Truth we know, we can no longer know the Truth *about* anything or anyone. Thus, all duality is transcended. Our boundless, indivisible *Isness* is our completeness. *Our Isness is our Oneness, and our Oneness is our Isness.* It is all "Being." It is all God being you. It is all you being God. The full and complete power that is knowledge will be perceived and evidenced constantly when wisdom and understanding are complete as knowledge. In this perception, all Truth is fully and completely perceived, and all Truth is fully and completely evidenced.

It is necessary to explore the Truth that is all knowledge quite extensively. This is particularly true of you who are now, or who will one day be,

Consultants in the Ultimate. Even if the Consultant activity does not seem to be your fulfillment of purpose at the moment, you will find that a persistent and consistent study and contemplation of the word *knowledge* will be tremendously inspiring and helpful in every aspect of your daily affairs and experiences. Oh yes, it is also helpful if any seeming inharmonious situation should arise concerning a bodily difficulty. In fact, there is no student of Absolute Truth who will not be immeasurably enlightened through the complete perception of what it means to know — and to know that you *are* what you know. And if you are engaged in the activity of being a Consultant, your perception that the one who has asked for help is both the knower and the Truth that is known is of the utmost importance.

Let us proceed with our exploration of the important word *knowledge*. Suppose you have just received a call for help. Right now you are aware of the fact that you are Omniscience, or all knowledge. Thus you perceive that you do know any Truth and every Truth that should be perceived. But don't stop with this perception. Realize also that the one who has called is this same Omniscience, which is all knowledge, and that he or she already knows any truth and every Truth that should be known at the moment.

Another aspect of your knowing should be that you *are* every Truth that you know. But it is vitally important to also realize that the one who has called is every Truth that you know and that he, being full knowledge, knows that he is the complete Truth. In short, it is necessary to perceive the fact that the one who has asked for help is the same conscious Omniscience that you are. You are *one* indivisible Consciousness. Therefore, you are also the very same Consciousness that he is. This is exceedingly important when a call for help first comes in.

In this omniscient—all knowing—perception, you realize that you do not project a so-called treatment. You also realize that there is no one in need of help or healing. You do not affirm any Truth, nor do you deny any untruth. You simply know that which is true because you, as well as the so-called patient, are Omniscience, all knowledge. Above all, you do not attempt to change anything that seems to be imperfect into something that is perfect. Perfection already and constantly *is*. The only necessity is the clear, enlightened perception that Absolute Perfection *is*, and Perfection means perfect Substance as well as perfect Activity.

Now, of course, you are aware of this Identity who has called. He has *appeared* to need help, and he has called himself to your attention. Therefore, you are consciously aware of him. But being aware of him does not mean that you consider him to be a separate Consciousness. On the contrary, your very first, and most constant, perception is that the Consciousness that you are is boundless, immeasurable, and inseparable. Furthermore, you are consistently aware of the fact that the Consciousness that everyone constantly *is*, is this same boundless, immeasurable, indivisible Consciousness. You can no more ignore his call for help than you can ignore any seeming inharmony that might appear to be your experience.

What does take place as your Consciousness at this point? The power of full, complete knowledge takes place. The complete Omniscience that you are is the power that you are. And never leave out of your contemplation the conscious Love that you are. You see, without Love, there could be no power at all. Love is our inseparable Oneness. It is Love that is the inseparability of the Consciousness of the one who has called for help and the Consciousness that you are.

In this way, you perceive that the Truth you know and know your Self to be is also known by the one who has called, and he knows himself to be that Truth. In short, you are saying, "I AM THAT I AM." But you are also saying, "That I AM is the *I* that I am.

In this way, you perceive that you are not separate consciousnesses, even though you are specific Identities. You are simply distinct Identities of the same universal Consciousness. Perhaps a better way of saying it would be: you are the one total Infinite Identity, identifying Itself as the specific Identity. But the specific Identity is the infinite, indivisible Identity, even as the one indivisible, infinite Identity is the specific identity.

Knowing this to be true, it is impossible for you to know any Truth *about* him, nor do you know any Truth *for* him. Rather, you are aware of *being* the

Truth that he knows and that he *is*. And you know that he is aware of knowing and being the Truth that you know and are. Oh, there is tremendous power in this kind of knowing.

Of course, so-called problems may appear under many guises. For instance, it may seem that someone is in need or that he seeks employment. He may report that he is lonely, unhappy, sinful, or sick. Often he will tell you that he is fearful. Oh, all sorts of reports may be received. No matter what may be the nature of the seeming problem, the foregoing revelations are the basis for all your "seeing."

In your activity as a Consultant, it is essential for you to realize that *you are Completeness.* This is true because to perceive this great Truth means that you realize your Self to be *all the Truth there is.* In this way, you can perceive the fact that whatever Truth you should know, you do know. Why? Because *you are the sum total of all Truth, and you know what you are.* Furthermore, *you are every Truth that you know.* Thus, whatever Truth is necessary at any moment is already present *as* the Consciousness that you are.

Sometimes one will be called when death seems imminent. In this illusory situation, there almost always seems to be great fear. So it is necessary to realize the Presence of the Mind that is Love and that this one and only Perfect Mind knows no fear and nothing to fear. It is impossible that Life should depart from Itself. The very Body Itself consists of eternal Life, and eternal Life cannot live temporarily.

Eternal Life does not enter Its own Substance, Body, nor can It depart from Its Substance, Body.

There is no coming and no going; no beginning and no ending. Life is omnipresent because Life is Omnipresence, constantly and without interruption. The living Substance, Body, must be as eternal as the Life Itself because the living Substance, Body, *is* eternal Life manifested in and as Form.

This does not mean that the Substance in Form, Body, is a separate part of Life. Rather, it is because Life is inseparable that the living Substance in Form is eternal. As you continue in the study of the Truths revealed in these pages, you will clearly understand how it is that Life, which is Substance, can be manifested as Form and yet be indivisibly the universal Life that is God.

There is another aspect of eternal Life that it is well to perceive when the illusion called death seems to threaten. This is the eternality of the Substance in Form of the specific Body Itself. Of course, this perception of the eternal Body also means the eternality of the specific Identity himself. Never, not even for a moment in the eternality of the Identity, is the Identity bodiless. Always the Identity and the Body are One.

This is true because the Identity *is* the Body, even as the Body *is* the Identity. The Body is necessary to the Completeness of the Identity, and if, for one moment, the Identity could be bodiless, in that moment he would be incomplete. There is never an excess, nor is there a deficiency of Substance in the Entirety that is the infinite Substance. Neither is there an excess nor a deficiency in the Entirety that is the Identity. This Truth precludes the possibility of either the beginning or the ending of the Body. Completeness is a universal Truth, or Fact. Completeness is an omnipresent Fact.

In the foregoing revelations, it is obvious that an illusory misconception—misperception—called matter never gave Life to the Identity, nor can this nonsubstance called matter take Life from the Identity. Eternal Life always manifests Itself as that which is alive, and that which is alive eternally is the Body.

There are many Truths that we perceive when it *appears* that Life is threatened. One of the most important of these omnipotent Truths is the fact that Life is eternally and infinitely Self-maintaining and Self-sustaining. No one should feel that he or she is responsible for sustaining or maintaining Life. Life is God, and God needs no help in order to be eternal Life. Our only responsibility is steadfast perception of the forever fact that God *is* All, All is God. It matters not what aspect of Truth we are contemplating; it remains God being That and That being God.

Here is just one more statement of Absolute Truth pertaining to eternal Life. We have stated that Life could not depart from the Substance that Life is. If it were possible for Life to depart from the Body, where would it go? And if this impossibility could be possible, would not the departure of Life leave a vacuum? *Life is omnipresent, for Life is Omnipresence.* There is never a vacuum in the Infinitude that is Life. Never is there a vacuum in the *one and only Mind* that knows Itself to be eternal Life. It is an absolute fact that the Mind that is eternal Life cannot know or be aware of death.

It may *seem* that you are not manifesting some aspect of the Truth you know, and know your Self to be. Of course, we cannot present or follow any method in our contemplation. Therefore, we can only speak in generalities on this subject. But it is helpful to perceive the fact that the Truth *is* true, even though you may not seem to be aware of It or to be evidencing Its Truth.

It may appear that your business is not going well or that your home is inharmonious. It may appear that you are lonely or a misfit. Oh, all sorts of illusions can seem to present themselves as your experience. However, these so-called problems that seem to be most prevalent are fallacious appearances pertaining to the body. No matter what the false picture may seem to be, it is always sheer illusion, and thus, it is nothing. But in case it seems true as far as you are concerned, what are you going to do about it? Are you going to know some Truth *about* your Self or *for* your Self? If so, you are going to seem to be separate from the Truth you know. But if you are aware of the fact that you *are* the Truth you know, you will find no false sense of separation between the Truth that you know and the Truth that you everlastingly *are*.

Truly, there is no Truth that is separate from you. There is no Truth other than the Truth you know, and know your Self to be. It is impossible to stress too strongly the necessity of knowing:

> You really are every Truth you know. You are every Truth that can be known.

Chapter VII

Clarification of Morning versus Evening Sessions

Right at this point, it seems necessary to clarify some aspects pertaining to our morning sessions versus our evening sessions.

Incidentally, this first volume of classwork presents the revelations of our morning sessions. You will note that these sessions are titled "The Omnipresent Omniactive I that I Am," while the evening sessions are titled "The I that I Am, Evidenced." Volume number two of this classwork is the Truth as revealed during our evening sessions.

There is wonderful completeness revealed as these two volumes. Yet it must be said that the revelations came in such a way that this first volume is quite complete, and this same Truth is true as the second volume of the classwork. It is just that each volume fulfills a specific purpose.

You will find that in this first volume we explore the Truth we are from the universal standpoint, while in the second volume we continue our discoveries of the universal Truth that is revealed in this first volume. However, in the second volume, we are decidedly specific in our "seeing." The word *evidenced* in the title of the second volume points up the fact that the evidence is the revelation of Absolute Truth manifested in, and as, your *specific* experience.

Truth experienced is evidence. The way in which these Truths, as presented in the two volumes, are being revealed is right in keeping with our entire approach as students of the Ultimate. In all our perception, our first approach is always from the universal standpoint, but if some seeming problem appears to be specific, we also perceive this Truth from the specific standpoint. As we have often stated, when the evidence of any Truth is apparent, it is a specific, as well as a universal, experience.

Now let us perceive some of these universal Truths that are specifically evidenced when we are aware of being the Truth we know.

For instance, let us realize the fact that Life is a universal Truth. *Every Truth is a universal, constant Truth.* Thus, Life is eternal, constant, and everywhere present. You are alive, and there is nothing alive but Life Itself. You are the Truth, and this means that you are the specific Truth that is universal, omnipresent, constant Life. How could this eternal Life that you are ever be threatened, come to an end, or die? It can't and you know It can't. The Truth that you are is universal, eternal, constant, ever-present Life. You can no more be separated from this Life than you can be separated from the Identity that you are. Your very Identity Itself is the Truth that you are. You are the Truth identified. You are *every* Truth identified. This absolute fact — that you never can be separated from the Truth that is Life—means that you will not, and cannot, die.

Just consider the power of this kind of knowing. It is the Power that is the entire Universe Itself, known and manifested as the very living Identity that you are this moment and eternally. Thus, Life is the Truth that you are, and you are the Truth that is Life. Thus, you can say, as did Jesus, "I am the truth … I am the life."

Jesus knew—and knows—that he is every Truth that he knows. When he said, "I am the way," he meant that the way to consciously *be* the evidence of this Truth is complete knowledge. And complete knowledge is your awareness of the fact that you *are* every Truth that you know and that you know every Truth that you are. There could be no complete knowledge *of* Truth unless you are aware that *you are the Truth Itself.* Now you can perceive the tremendous importance of Jesus' statement, "I am the truth, the life, and the way." Is it any wonder the Bible says, "Let that mind be in you that was also in Christ Jesus."

Chapter VIII

The Nature of Illusion

Our next step in the realization of what we genuinely are must, of necessity, be the perception of what we are not. This is indeed a paradox. Nonetheless, our recognition of what we are not does strengthen and clarify our perception of that which we really are.

This is not affirmation and denial. Rather, it is only because we know so well that which is true that we can consider that which is not true in such perfect, peaceful equanimity. Every day we are faced with these apparent imperfections and problems. Make no mistake about it, it certainly is helpful to be capable of perceiving just what they are and, of course, to perceive just why they are not what they seem to be at all. It is our knowledge of that which is genuine that reveals why these seeming inharmonies simply are not, and cannot, be.

Often the question is asked, "What is illusion?" or, "What is evil?" Actually, illusion, or evil, is nothing. Frequently we will hear someone say, "Oh, I know this is not real." There is no such thing as a real and an unreal substance or activity. That which is genuine is all that exists. That which is genuine is eternal and omnipresent. Perhaps it is just as well to define evil, or illusion, as ignorance.

But one might ask, "What is ignorance?" In our use of the word *ignorance*, we do not mean stupidity. Ignorance, if such were possible, would be lack of knowledge. Of course, this would imply an absence of the Mind that is complete, or *all* knowledge. But this all-knowing Mind is Omnipresence, so there can be no absence of knowledge. Therefore, that which is called evil, or illusion, would have to be an absence of Mind rather than the Omnipresence that *is* Mind. Therefore, evil, or illusion, is nothing. There is no evil. There is no absence of the Mind that is all knowledge. The presence of Mind precludes the possibility of such a thing as an absence of Mind. The omnipresent Mind that is all knowledge cannot be present and also be absent.

It is true that sometimes illusory nothingness does appear to exist. A very clear explanation of just how this enigma can even seem to be is found in the book *You Are the Splendor*. If you will begin at the second paragraph, page 157, and study to the end of the first paragraph on page 170, you will certainly perceive how it is, and why it is, that evil, illusion, can *seem* to be something that it is not. A thorough study and contemplation of the Truths revealed on these pages will enable you to realize that even an illusion that appears to be evil simply signifies the presence of the Good, or God, that genuinely *is*. [Editor's note: The excerpt from *You Are the Splendor* is included at the end of this chapter for the reader's convenience.]

Oh, yes, sometimes it seems that so-called evil has, or is, power. How could ignorance have or be power? How could an absence of Mind — if this were possible — be power? Mind, Intelligence, full knowledge, is *Power*, and this all-knowing Mind is the only Presence. Suppose it appears that the Substance in Form called your Body seems to be diseased or deteriorating. How could an absence of conscious, living Mind be Substance? It can't. It isn't. Then, too, it may appear that some aspect of the Body is not acting perfectly or functioning as it should. How could an absence of Mind be active? Only that which is present can act. That which is present is the *only* Power.

There is only one word that states clearly and completely *all that exists*, and this word is *God.* No matter how glorious or how abundant are our revelations, it is all God revealing Itself. But to whom is God revealing Itself? There is no one other than God, so it is God revealing Itself *to* Itself *as* Itself. And this Self is the *I* Self that *you* are.

Let us again briefly discuss some general aspects of the activity of the Consultant. Of course, we do not give treatments because we know that there is nothing that needs to be healed or changed. Naturally, God — Perfection — being the *only One*, we know that there is no one in need of help or healing or treatment. But we do respond when a call for help is received. Furthermore, if something *seems* to be inharmonious in and as our own experience or our Body, we do perceive and contemplate, specifically as well as universally, that which is true, or Truth. We do not know a Truth and then deny an untruth, or error. Rather, we simply contemplate that which *is* true, realizing that there is nothing opposite to contemplate.

We may contemplate in the following manner:

Beyond all mesmerism or delusion, God *is. I am That.* Beyond all false laws of illusion, God is. *I am That.* Beyond all supposed birth, change, or death, God is. *I am That.* Beyond all the fallacies of age, deterioration, or infirmities, God is. *I am That.* Beyond all illusory memories of a human past, God is. *I am That.* Beyond all illusions of time or space, God is. *I am That.* Beyond all illusions of imperfection, God is. *I am That.*

Beyond all falsities of fear or dread, God is. *I am That.* Beyond all delusions of sickness, suffering, or disease, God is. *I am That.* Beyond all appearances of imperfect activity, God is. *I am That.* Beyond all seeming depletion or augmentation, God is. *I am That.* Beyond all illusions of imperfect substance or activity, God is. *I am That.* Beyond all so-called laws of a supposedly born body, God is. *I am That.* Beyond all false appearance of a body of matter, bone, blood, nerves, and sinew, God is. *I am That.*

Beyond all misconceptions of a human mind in a born brain, God is. *I am That.* Beyond all fictitious laws of heredity, God is. *I am That.* Beyond all mistaken laws of time or space, God is. *I am That.* Beyond all fallacious laws of evolution, God is. *I am That.* Beyond all so-called ages of accumulated beliefs, fears, habits, or characteristics, God is. *I am That.*

Beyond all supposed struggle and strife of assumptive man, God is. *I am That.* Beyond all delusions of hate or destruction, God is. *I am That.* Beyond all apparent loneliness or sorrow, God is. *I am That.* Beyond all seeming anger, resistance, or effort, God is. *I am That.* Beyond all appearances of opposites, God is. *I am That.* Beyond all false sense of twoness or separation, God is. *I am That.* Beyond all apparent inharmony of any nature, God is. *I am That.*

If this contemplation has to do with one who has called for help, you may prefer to substitute the words *Thou art* for the words *I am.* In any event, the meaning is the same. As this enlightened Consciousness, you may now say:

Thine is—thus I am—the kingdom, the power, and the glory. Thou art—thus I am— exalted as head above all. Thou art—thus I am— all knowledge, all understanding, all Life, all Love. All thine are mine, and mine are thine; for we are one perfect, eternal, infinite, indivisible One.

Oh, there is tremendous power in these statements of Truth when the full and complete import of their spiritual significance is realized. You see, it is all in the one word, *God.* No cold intellectualism can intrude when the true spirit of this word, *God,* is perceived, felt, and experienced. This is particularly true when we realize the unalterable Truth that *we are That* and that *this one and only I that I am is the entirety of our being.*

There are no affirmations and denials here. There is an acknowledgment that evil *seems* to be, but there is an immediate perception of the Truth that *is* rather than the illusion that is not. Yes, beyond all the appearances of anything separate from, or other than, God, *you are the all-knowing Mind that is eternally and infinitely the Light.* Beloved, all of this is just another way of saying:

I know every Truth that I am. I am every Truth that I know.

As you know, all revelation is Self-revelation. In like manner, all contemplation of Truth must reveal itself as the Consciousness that *you* are. This being true, it naturally follows that perhaps the identical words may not be the words that will be revealed as the Consciousness that you are. Just silently contemplate and *let* the words come as they will. Whatever words you hear or sense will be those that are right as your revelation at the moment.

Actually, you may find that many more statements than those presented here are literally surging and flowing as your awareness. The important aspect of all contemplation is that you clearly perceive that it is all the God-Consciousness revealing Itself *to* Itself as Itself — *and this Self is your Self.*

There can be no method and no set procedure for contemplation. Infinite, boundless, eternal, omniscient

Mind *always* knows what should be perceived and perceives it. You can trust this limitless Mind that you are to reveal Itself as any Truth that is essential at any moment. However, there is one fact that I am very sure you will discover to be true—namely, that the foregoing statements of Absolute Truth present the *basis* of all true revelation. What is this basis? *God is All, All is God.*

[Editor's note: The following excerpt is from the book *You Are the Splendor*, Chapter 10, pp. 157-170 (published by Mystics of the World) to which the author referred on page 58 of this chapter.]

Let us now perceive how it is, and why it is, that any *appearance* of evil is *not* evil—that it really serves a good purpose. If the fulfillment of any purpose is good, the impulsion behind this purpose has to be good and not evil. The mistake lies in our misconception of the meaning of that which we have called evil.

A mistake in mathematics is due to momentary ignorance of the perfect fact or principle of mathematics. An awareness of the perfect principle instantly corrects the mistake. The mistake has served to call your attention to the figure or figures that are right.

For instance, in solving a mathematical problem, it is possible to mistakenly write the figure 5 when the figure 4 should be written. This mistake will be evident throughout the entire procedure. Thus, the answer will be false, or untrue. Once the mistake is discovered, you are no longer concerned with it. Rather, you are concerned only with that which is right and true, namely the figure 4. But the mistake has called your attention to the perfect mathematical principle. Thus, the mistake has fulfilled a definite purpose.

Just as a mistake in mathematics calls your attention to the perfect mathematical fact, so it is that any appearance of evil serves to call your attention to some specific aspect of good, or God. God is Perfection; thus, Perfection is a universal as well as a specific fact. Any appearance of imperfection serves to call your attention to the perfect Principle, which is Perfection. *A mistake can seem to be troublesome or evil only so long as it is mistaken for a fact.* Once your attention is focused upon the perfect fact, the mistake is canceled. It simply vanishes.

Perfection is a universal fact. Imperfection is *not* a universal fact. Perfection is the specific fact. Imperfection is *not* the specific fact. Any appearance of imperfection but serves to focus your attention upon the Perfection which *does* exist. You know that only that which is a universal fact can be a specific fact.

You do not resist the mistake. You do not attempt to overcome it or to oppose it. You know it to be a mistake, and that ends it as far as you are concerned. The mistake has served its purpose, and your attention is now focused upon the perfect Principle. You keep your attention focused upon the universal and the specific fact until the evidence of this fact is apparent. You can never make a figure 5 become a figure 4. Neither can you make an appearance of imperfection become perfect. Your awareness of Perfection is the revelation and the evidence of that which is revealed.

Sickness, pain, disease, discord of any kind are not existent. They are not evidence of the perfect fact. Each is only an illusory appearance which serves to call your attention to the omnipresent fact which *does* exist. In this same way, apparent lack, trouble, or discord of any nature calls your attention to the universal Principle of supply, peace, joy, or harmony.

If you continue to be concerned with an appearance of discord, your attention remains focused upon a mistake. It is focused upon that which has already served its purpose and should be dismissed. So long as your attention continues to be focused upon a discordant appearance, that illusory appearance will continue to appear to be genuine. When you are constantly and consciously attentive to the perfect fact—*and only this fact*—the evidence of its presence is inevitable.

"Thou wilt keep him in perfect peace, whose mind is stayed on thee: because he trusteth in thee" (Isa. 26:3). To keep the attention constantly stayed on God is to hold firmly to the perfect Principle, or the existing fact. It is necessary to keep the attention focused upon the perfect fact if you are to have complete trust in God. *God is the perfect Fact.* God is the Entirety of your Existence, so the perfect Principle is your own Identity, your Life, your Consciousness, your Intelligence, and your Body. If you keep your Consciousness stayed on God, you are continuously aware of the Perfection which constitutes all there is of you. Perfection is omnipresent, so It remains present right where and when any appearance of discord calls your attention to its presence.

If apparent evil serves to draw your attention to God, or Good, then apparent evil is not evil, but good. It is God—who comprises your entire Existence—revealing Its Omnipresence. It makes no difference what the specific appearance of evil may be; the specific fact is already established in and as your own Consciousness. Your attention is simply being called to the specific fact. Thus, any appearance of evil must be but a signal signifying the presence of God, Good, Perfection. Now you perceive the truth of the statement, "There is no evil." You also realize why this statement is true.

The appearance of a material universe signifies the presence of the Universe of Light, or Spirit. The appearance of solidity signifies the presence of the Essence which is spiritual. An appearance of density, or darkness, signifies the presence of Light. The appearance of stupidity signifies the presence of Intelligence. In like manner, any appearance of temporal life, mind, consciousness signifies the presence of eternal Life, Intelligence, Consciousness.

The appearance of a personal "I"—assumptive man—signifies the presence of God evidencing Itself as the Identity. The assumptive "born body" signifies the eternal Body, comprised of Life, Mind, Consciousness. The assumption that there is a human mind centered in a brain signifies the presence of infinite Intelligence, specifically identified. The appearance of a human consciousness, or life, is the signal announcing the presence of the infinite, eternal, conscious Life, identified as the specific conscious Life. That which is called human activity signifies the infinite Universe in action, or Omniaction, identified as specific activity. Our task is to keep the attention centered upon the universal, as well as the specific, Existence which is being signified.

Now let us perceive in what way this explanation of the signal, miscalled evil, may be helpful in our experience. We know that it is impossible to follow a method in this approach, so we will not consider the following to be a formula. Nevertheless, we can base our general contemplation upon the Truths that are here revealed, and we know that the right answers will be revealed within and as our own God-Consciousness. Certain it is that every statement you have read or are going to read here is absolute Truth.

We have said that any appearance of discord is but the signal for the infinite, eternal Perfection which is forever an established fact. We have realized that any fact that is a universal fact is a specific fact. We can now perceive the natural revelation and the evidence of the universal, yet specific, fact in the following way.

Suppose, for instance, you seem to be the victim of hatred or injustice. You know that any appearance of hatred would be the opposite of Love. You know that Love exists; thus, hatred does *not* exist. So the illusion called hatred is but the signal calling your attention to the presence of that which *does* exist, namely Love.

You do not dwell on the illusion, the signal, because it of itself is nothing. But you do not resist the signal. Neither do you oppose it. Rather, you focus your attention entirely upon the universal — and specific — fact which *does* exist. And this fact is: God is Love. Yes, God is Love universally. God is Love specifically. You contemplate the innumerable and various ways in which this infinite Love is apparent as the perfect harmony of this Universe. You consider the wonderful way in which each star and planet fulfills its purpose in perfect harmony with the stars and planets which constitute this galaxy. You realize that this perfect, harmonious activity is Love in action. You also realize that Love is Intelligence; therefore, this universal activity is Intelligence acting lovingly. In this way, you have perceived the *impersonal* nature of Love. You have also realized that Love is a universal Truth, or fact.

Now, you may consider the perfect way in which our own Earth planet functions. The harmonious activity of this planet is perfect Love in action. *This same Love in action is all that is active in and as your experience.* This is being specific. This is realizing that universal, perfect Love is active in and as your specific existence. There is nothing to oppose this omnipotent, omniactive, perfect Love, and there is no one existing who can resist It. But this is not all; there is no one who is genuinely conscious of anything that is contrary or opposite to this perfect, universal, infinite Love.

Your Consciousness is your Universe. This means that only that which comprises your Consciousness can be present, or evident, in or as your Life, your Consciousness, and your daily experience. Love alone is revealed as your Consciousness, so Love—and *only* Love—can be evidenced as your specific existence. This means that you are *not* aware of a supposititious opposite of Love, called hatred, in your daily affairs.

During this contemplation, you are intently alert. You do not permit an illusion of inactivity seemingly to put you to sleep. Neither do you aimlessly drift into an indifferent, indolent attitude. This is an active Truth.

During your contemplation of infinite Love will come a point at which a tremendous sense of peace and joy floods your entire Consciousness. But don't cease contemplating at this point. Joy is the harbinger of Love. Continue in your contemplation until you experience that great omnipotent surge of infinite Love. This is the apex of all your "seeing." Having reached this glorious height, you may now rest assured that you are truly seeing things as they are.

You may rest in this true perception, but you will not let your attention be distracted. You will not investigate to see whether or not the perfect fact, Love, is completely evidenced. You will not concern yourself with the signal—the seeming evil—again. You will "keep your mind stayed on God." You will discover that the Truth you have been perceiving is present; It is all that is, ever has been, or ever will be present. But best of all, you will discover that the Truth you have perceived is *evident* right here and right now. Furthermore, the evidence will be all that *is* apparent, and it will be all that you are conscious of seeing or experiencing. Then it will appear that a healing has taken place. But you will know better. You will know that you have simply seen Existence as It is, and *the signal to draw your attention to this fact need never again appear.*

You have noted that we have gone quite thoroughly into the basic approach to the realization of Love, harmony, justice, perfection in your experience. There is nothing nebulous about this approach. It is most clear-cut and definite. Yet it must be revealed within and as your own Consciousness, and it will be *your own* revelation. However, it must be said that this same basic approach can be followed in every situation where inharmony of any kind appears.

It may be that an appearance of lack seems to be present. This is not evil. Rather, it should be considered as merely the signal signifying the presence of infinite, omnipresent Supply. You will not approach this aspect of existence from the standpoint of the specific. Instead you will immediately contemplate the universal fact, which is omnipresent Supply. This is a complete Universe. Its completeness precludes the possibility that anything could be missing that is necessary to Its Allness, Its Entirety. The realization of completeness is of vital importance in every situation where incompleteness, or lack, appears to be evident.

Actually, incompleteness, or lack, would seem to prevail in any illusion of trouble, disorder, or inharmony. It might appear as a lack of health, a lack of strength, a lack of joy or peace, or a lack of supply in the aspect called money. In any event, realization of the presence of that which *appears* to be absent is necessary if you are to experience the evidence of complete supply. Thus, it is apparent why the word *completeness* is of such vital importance.

Completeness is a universal fact. Thus, Supply is a universal fact. It is present everywhere, and It is present eternally. There are no vacuums in this universal fact, and there is no interruption of Its Presence. It is indivisible. It is that Principle which is omnipresent and inseparable from the specific Identity, which is God identified as you. It is within your Consciousness because It is constituted of your Consciousness. If you will realize that Supply, in any aspect, is as omnipresent as is Love, you will perceive the true nature of Supply. If you will "keep your mind stayed" on the presence of Supply —

God—you will surely be aware of the evidence of this Presence right here and now.

Suppose a feeling of frustration or inadequacy seems to persistently present itself. It may appear that you are not fulfilling your purpose. It may seem that your activity is too limited or that your supply is limited by your present work or profession. Here again, it is essential to recognize the signal, then immediately to perceive the universal fact. This is an intelligent Universe. The Intelligence which comprises this perfect Universe is omniactive. Omniactive Intelligence acts intelligently, and thus It constantly fulfills Its purpose.

> The universal purpose of omniactive Intelligence is the eternal, infinite maintenance and sustenance of absolute Perfection.

God, the Universe, is Self-maintained and Self-sustained. God, omniactive Intelligence, is ever active, maintaining Itself as eternal Perfection.

Your activity is inseparable from universal Omniaction. It can no more be an isolated activity than the activity of the wave can be isolated from the ceaseless movement of the ocean. The fulfillment of your purpose in being can never be divided from the purposeful fulfillment of the universal purpose. The fulfillment of purpose is universal, but it is also specific. The specific activity is essential to the completeness which is Omniaction. Therefore, your activity is absolutely necessary, and the fulfillment of your purpose in being is essential to the complete fulfillment of the universal completeness—the Totality which is God.

If it appears that you are not adequately fulfilling your purpose in being, this appearance can mean only that your attention has been called to this specific aspect of your completeness. The appearance of frustration signifies the presence of infinite fulfillment. It means that right here and now you are to perceive and to evidence the limitless fulfillment of your purpose in being. Consider these Truths. Consider them from the universal standpoint, then from the specific standpoint. If you will continue in this contemplation, you will find that your opportunities are limitless, and your profession, or work, is satisfying and fulfilling.

Sometimes it will seem that a decision must be made. It will appear that you do not know what course to pursue in some situation. This merely signifies that infinite Intelligence is present right here and now. It means that this omniactive Intelligence knows how to act and acts intelligently.

This is apparent when you consider the Perfection manifested as the omniactive Universe. There is no indecision, no wondering what to do, evident in the universal intelligent activity. The infinite Mind which acts knows how to act, when to act, and *acts*. The universal Mind in action is the Mind which is your Intelligence. The Intelligence that knows what Its activity should be, and *is*, is in full and complete operation as your own Intelligence right here and now. Had the answer not been already present, no question as to what course you should take would have arisen. In other words, the question is the signal that the answer is present within and as your Consciousness, insisting upon being revealed and evidenced.

Suppose that which is miscalled evil appears as symptoms of age, of change, of deterioration, or something that has to do with an aging mind or body. This appearance is exceedingly significant. It signifies the presence of beginningless, changeless, endless Existence. It signifies the universal fact that God, the Universe, is without beginning, change, or ending. It signifies the universal Consciousness of this fact. It signifies the fact that Life is eternal and imperishable and that the perfect Essence of all existence is indestructible. It is the signal for you to — recognize the Eternality of your Life, Being, and Body. It means that eternity is now, and infinity is here. It means that the universal, imperishable Identity is being revealed as *your* Identity.

But this is not all. The signal has announced that *you* are the presence of the beginningless, changeless, endless Essence, and you are conscious of being this Essence. Therefore, you are aware of being the evidence of the universal fact which is revealing Itself as all there is of you. The Universe has not aged. The Universe has not deteriorated. Neither is It in the process of being destroyed. That which has been revealed as a universal Truth is true as your very Existence. You are this Truth, and you know it. Your knowing of this fact is the evidence of the Truth you know your Self to be.

Any unsatisfied longing signifies the presence of the satisfying and perfect fact. It may appear that you yearn for human satisfaction of some kind. But this seeming yearning is but the signal drawing your attention to the presence of the spiritual fact which satisfies. The presence of that which satisfies is your own divine Consciousness, aware of being eternally complete, lacking nothing that is essential to Its completeness.

A dinner bell is the signal announcing that the food is already prepared and you are free to partake of it. In this same way, any appearance of inharmony is but a signal announcing the presence of any perfect fact that is necessary to your complete harmony, perfection, and freedom. The dinner bell is not important of itself. It is not the food. Yet it signifies the presence of the food. You do not resist or resent the sound of the ringing of this bell. Rather you welcome it and act accordingly.

Suppose you misunderstood the sound of the bell. Suppose you misinterpreted it, and to you it signified danger or some horrendous event. In this case, you might appear to be fearful, angry, or resentful. Yet if you were to discover the true meaning of the signal, the fear, anger, or resentment would immediately disappear. Furthermore, the illusion of danger or anything of a catastrophic nature would have vanished. Above all, you would have discovered the genuine Presence — and the nature of the Presence — of that which the dinner bell signified. In other words, enlightened Consciousness reveals the Perfection which *is*, rather than the assumed imperfection which is *not*.

[End of Excerpt]

Chapter IX

Oneness Is the Christ

God, being Man, is the Christ. But the Christ, being Man, is also God. Herein is our completeness and our complete Oneness. For instance, when we say, "God is All" and then instantly complete the statement by saying, "All is God," we have really stated the Oneness, the identicalness of all Existence. Somehow, just to say "God is All" does not seem complete unless we also state that "All is God." "God is All" states that God is all Substance, all Life, all Mind, Consciousness, all Love, all Activity. Then to state that "All is God" signifies that all Substance, all Life, all Mind, Consciousness, all Love, all Activity are God.

You can perceive how it is, and why it is, that this is a perfect statement of completeness. You will find it helpful to perceive every statement as completeness in this way. Being aware of the Truth of the foregoing statements, you will find that the revelations that follow are tremendously enlightening in and as the Consciousness that you are. So let us repeat: God, being Man, is the Christ. The Christ, being Man, is God.

The Body of God, being the Body of Man, is the Christ-Body. The Body of Man, being the Christ-Body, is the Body of God. The Mind that is God, being the Mind of Man, is the Christ-Mind. The Christ-Mind, being the Mind that is Man, is the Mind that is God. The God-Consciousness, being the Consciousness of Man, is the Christ-Consciousness. The Christ-Consciousness, being the Consciousness of Man, is the God-Consciousness. The Life that is God, being the Life that is Man, is the Christ-Life, or the living Christ. The Life that is Man, being the living Christ, is the Life that is God, or *the living God*. The Love that is God, being the Love that is Man, is the Christ-Love. The Love that is Man, being the loving Christ, is the Love that is God.

Oh, Beloved, can you see how it is, and why it is, that God, the Christ, and you are inseparably One Essence, One Mind, One Consciousness, One Life, One Love? Can you see how it is, and why it is, that *you are the temple of the living God and that the temple of the Life that is God is you?* Can you see that this glorious revelation completely obliterates any fallacious sense of separateness, twoness, or of duality? Can you see how it is, and why it is, that God, the Christ, and *You* are the very same identical One? Of course you can, and you can realize clearly what Jesus meant when he said, "I and the Father are one" — that he also indicated that the Father and he were one.

The Christ-Body, or the Body of the Christ, is the eternal, perfect, ever changeless Body that was never born, nor can It ever die. Neither can It be or become imperfect or deteriorate. The revelation of this fact is the *only* resurrection, and this resurrection is going on right here and right now, as you read and contemplate these words of Absolute Truth. Rightly understood, the Resurrection is the *revelation* of the eternal, perfect, changeless Body of Light. But the Resurrection is also the revelation, through illumination, of the boundless Universe, which is the infinite, boundless Body of God. Furthermore, this boundless Body of God is the universal Consciousness that you are. And the universal Consciousness that you are is the infinite, immeasurable, boundless Body of God.

In other words, the universal Consciousness that you are is the universal Body that you are. This Substance in Form, right here, called your Body, is your universal Consciousness focused, embodied, right here at the moment. But always know that it is the universal Consciousness that is manifested as this Substance in Form right here and now.

This Body is the universal Consciousness you are, fulfilling Its purpose as Body, right here and now, as this specific Body. This Body right here is the specific embodiment of the universal Body. Thus, Its Essence, or Substance, is identically the same Essence that comprises the boundless, eternal, perfect Universe, which is God. There just isn't anything — any Substance — that can be embodied other than the universal Substance, which is the universal Body. And there is no activity that can possibly go on in or as this embodiment here that is not being active in and as the activity of the Universal Body.

This Universe is a living, ever-moving, breathing Substance. It is vitally, dynamically alive. Its Substance is Life Itself, and this universal Substance is always in Form. In all of boundless infinity, there is no Substance without Form. There is no formless substance. The physicists who are engaged in the space program know that the very air is comprised of structural atoms. Well, a structure is form, isn't it? For that matter, that which is called an atom exists in and as form. Yes, every so-called proton, electron, neutron, and even every nucleus, exists as form.

Now, don't be deceived; we are not speaking of matter or of matter in form. But there *is* something here that is called the atom, and we are to clearly perceive just what this something is. In our evening classes, which comprise the second volume of this classwork, we shall thoroughly explore the true Nature of that which is called the atom. But it is sufficient just now to perceive that the Substance in Form called the atom does exist and that this Substance is *not* matter. Rather, It is Consciousness, Life, Mind, Love—and of course, all of this is *Light*. Spirit

We do not ordinarily see these atomic structures that comprise the atmosphere. I say "ordinarily" because there are some enlightened ones who have seen, and do see, the atmospheric Substance in Form that the physicists call atomic structures. Those of you who have experienced this vision of the true

Nature of the air will understand our assertions. But although these seeming atmospheric Forms do appear invisible to most of us, almost everyone accepts the physicists' explanation of this fact.

Now, here is a paradox. Even the so-called man in the street is willing to believe that there is atmospheric substance in form, although he cannot actually see it; yet when we speak of the Body of Light, which is generally invisible, we meet with skepticism or ridicule.

What is the difference between the seemingly invisible atmospheric Substance in Form and the apparently invisible Substance in Form that is the Body of Light? Actually there is no difference at all because all Substance is the same identical Substance. Furthermore, that which appears to be visible to the admittedly human vision is not really Substance; it is only an appearance. It is merely the way Substance appears to this befuddled, illusory, completely fallacious vision of born man with breath in his nostrils. Wouldn't it seem that if we can accept the physicists' statements that the seemingly invisible Forms—atomic structures—do exist, that we should also be able, willingly, to accept the statement that the seemingly invisible structure—Body of Light—does exist?

Throughout the ages, there have been enlightened ones who have seen the Body of Light. Indeed, more of us are seeing this Body of Light than ever before. Incidentally, several of the students in this class have reported seeing the Body of Light right here, and once this Body of Light is seen, no one can convince the enlightened "see-er" that It does not exist. He knows better.

There will come a day when everyone will see this Body of Light, and that, beloved ones, will mean the complete end of the tragic illusion called death. But this is not all. It will also be the end of the delusion called birth. It will be the end of war, destruction, and all that has seemed to plague us throughout what seemed to be dark centuries.

Light is all Substance. All Substance is Light. All Substance exists in and as Form. Thus, all Substance in and as Form is Light. Form is a structure and a structure is a body. From the foregoing, you can perceive that every Form is a Body of Light. Full illumination always reveals this Universe to be Light and nothing but Light. And now we can understand just why this glorious infinity of Light is always perceived in full enlightenment. However, it must be said now that sometimes—not always—the Light is so gloriously brilliant that It seems to conceal the innumerable Forms in and as which It exists. Nonetheless, we are always aware of the fact that there is Form. It is in this way that we realize the eternality of the Body.

It is the Body of Light that is beginningless, changeless, endless. It is the Body of Light that is imperishable and indestructible. And, Beloved One, this is the only Body in existence right here and now as the Body of You, of Everyone.

Chapter X

The Universal Ocean of Living Light

Now, lest we seem to go too far afield, let us return to our Universe and Its Activity. We find that it is necessary to frequently reconsider Truth from the universal standpoint. This is true because the only way we can know — thus consciously be — what our Substance and Activity *are* is to perceive what the universal Substance and Activity are and to perceive the Nature of the universal Substance and Its Activity. You will realize, of course, that when we speak of the Universe, we are speaking of boundless Infinity.

Often we speak of Infinity as the Universe because, for our *practical* purpose here and now, the word *Universe* is more suitable. This Absolute Truth, perceived and experienced, is indeed practical. What would be the use of all our glorious, enlightened experiences unless we perceived and experienced these Truths in action right where we seem to be focused at the moment?

Make no mistake about it, the Absolute Truths you are perceiving right now are practical. You will find that these Truths are present and *active* in and as every event of your daily Life and experience. But this is not all. You will find these Absolute Truths to be active in and as the entire Substance and Activity of this Body. Many students of the Ultimate are constantly aware of the Presence of this Truth and Its effortless, joyous activity in and as their daily lives and as the perfection of their Bodies and the bodily activity. Oh, you would rejoice if you were to read the letters we receive daily; or better yet, if you could hear the reports of those who joyously tell us of their effortless, joyous, successful activity. And of course, there are always reports of the dynamic, inexhaustible, perfect Body and Its Activity.

Just recently a wonderful couple arrived from Hawaii, and as they joyously spoke of their experiences, my Heart really leapt with joy. I wish that I could share all of their report with you, but this is impossible. I can tell you, though, that where there had formerly appeared to be frustration—this in spite of sincere striving to "know the Truth"—now there has dawned the full living Light which reveals that they *are* this Absolute Truth Itself. And of course, there is now no struggle, no anxiety, and certainly no Self-limitation of any kind.

Oh, it is such a joyous occasion to hear these glorious reports. And the outstanding aspect of the effortless, successful activity this couple is experiencing is the fact that they know they do not have to *do* anything of themselves in order that it take place.

You see, when you realize that you genuinely *are* every Truth you perceive, you find that you are not doing something of yourself. Rather, you are *being* this Truth, and you are being this Truth in action. In this way, you find that these wonderful things just take place, but there is no effort and certainly no struggle involved.

Now, where are these joyous, free experiences going on? Right within and *as* the Consciousness that is the Identity Itself. Nothing can take place, or be experienced, outside of the Consciousness of the Identity because there is no "outside." There is no place outside, or other than, the Consciousness that You are.

This brings us to one of the most powerful of our statements of Absolute Truth. You will find it in the book of classwork, *Three Essential Steps*. Here it is: *your Consciousness is your Universe*. Now let us complete this statement: *your Universe is your Consciousness.*

When you know what your Universe really is and know that you *are* your own Universe, even as your Universe is *you*, all perfect, joyous, free activity just goes on without any effort at all. However, this glorious, free, purposeful Life could never be consciously experienced if you continued to be deluded by the fabrication that you were separate born beings who were capable of doing something or of being someone as a little personal self. It simply cannot be realized and experienced this way. You see, it is in your awareness of the infinite, indivisible Nature of your Being that all these perfectly normal, effortless activities take place.

You will recall this significant statement in our Bible: "Not by might, nor by power, but by my spirit, saith the Lord of hosts" (Zech. 4:6). Yes, not by any separate so-called human effort, nor by mental might, nor by any personal, dualistic sense of power are these wonderfully fulfilling things realized and evidenced. Rather, it is by knowing and being the conscious, universal, indivisible Entirety Itself that all things move and act freely, joyously, and oh, so successfully. Actually, you discover that you *are* the Power. It is not that you have power over anything or anyone. Rather, it is that you *are* Power, just by knowing — knowledge — and by being the Truth that you know.

Very soon now, you will discover why it is that you have seemed to make such an effort to fulfill any purpose or to accomplish anything worthwhile. Perhaps the quotations from a letter recently received will help to clarify this point.

This letter is from a really fine artist who heretofore had not quite perceived that he was, and is, the Beauty that is Art, even as the Art that is Beauty is the Identity that he is.

> I got a very fair business offer from the man who is going to handle my pictures. (He flatters the work shamefully.) By the way, I discover the work itself has taken a big step forward, which I feel is due to my study and assimilation of *Success*

Is Normal. I notice that I am not afraid when I am painting, but plunge ahead with an absurd confidence. I don't seem to be so burdened with a sense of personal activity — or virtuosity. The painter is somewhat like a planchette. He has no movement of his own. The picture is already painted. It is, for me, fantastic to have the fear removed from the work. I have set the work free.

Isn't this wonderful? Actually, this enlightened Identity is perceiving that he *is* the eternal Beauty that is the painting and that the painting is the eternal Beauty that he is. It is true that the painting already existed. It is equally true that everything in existence is eternal *as what it is.* To "set the work (the manifested Beauty) free" means to perceive and to consciously *be* that which we perceive.

Now, in order to further clarify the universal *I* that you are, we will have to speak in similes. I wish that it were not necessary to do this, as similes are always faulty. Nonetheless, I am convinced that the following clarification, even though it is presented in similes, will prove to be the most revelatory of anything we have so far perceived.

All of us have seen streams, rivers, creeks, and the like. Most of us have observed that often, when the water reaches a certain point, it will circulate — sometimes quite rapidly — at that point and then flow along again as the stream itself. These focal points at which the water circulates, or goes in a circle, are called eddies, or whirlpools. It never occurs to us that the water of the eddy is confined *within* the form in which it circulates. Neither could we believe that the water circulating as the eddy was different from, or other than, the water that is the river itself.

Now, let us consider this Universe as though it were a *boundless* ocean of ever-moving, living Light. Let us perceive that this Light—which is Life—is constantly moving, flowing, and surging throughout and *as* its Entirety. We may also perceive that this Entirety is the universal—and *only*—Substance. Yes, it is important that we know this constantly living, moving Light to be Substance and that it is the only Substance in existence.

As we contemplate this boundless ocean of ever-living Light, we will assuredly realize that the activity of this Light, which is Life, is irresistible, unobstructible, and irrepressible. Indeed, we know that there is nothing existing that can resist, obstruct, or repress the omnipotent, omnipresent, infinite activity which is this Universe in action. The boundless ocean of living Light being all that exists, how could there be *anything* that could resist, oppose, repress, or obstruct Its constant, flowing, surging, circulating motion or activity?

It is essential now that we again refer to the simile of the eddy or the whirlpool. (However, as stated before, all similes are inadequate and faulty.) Referring to the material explanation of an eddy or whirlpool, it is said that an obstruction in the form of a stick, stone, or something like that obstructs the moving water temporarily, even though it circulates and then flows on. Let us be very sure that we do not accept as fact this so-called material appearance called an obstruction. For our purpose, it is necessary to completely disregard the so-called material explanation as to the cause of the eddy or whirlpool.

We do know that the water of the stream is constantly flowing *to* the eddy and that this water circulates in and as the eddy before it continues its movement as the water of the stream itself. It is noteworthy that the water of the eddy is identically the same as is the water of the stream itself. But, for completeness, we realize that the water of the stream itself is identically the same water that circulates in and as the eddy.

Right here is a paradox. Although the water of the eddy is constantly the water that is the stream, yet *the water of the eddy is constantly new water*. In other words, the water of the eddy is always the same, yet it is always new and fresh.

Now, for the purpose of clear perception, let us realize that there is never any accumulation of the water of the eddy, nor is there any diminution of this water. Always it remains the same, without one extra drop of water and without one drop of water being deleted. Of course, this would not actually be true of the so-called material stream, which appears to swell or to diminish according to the inflow of its tributaries or its outflow. But we are to perceive the immutable nature of all Substance, and for this purpose, we will disregard the seeming change in the volume of water. It is important that we perceive that there is never any more and never any less Substance as the eddy.

> God, Infinity, is ever complete, and never is there any more—not one iota more—or less of the Completeness which is God. Furthermore, God, the infinite ocean of living Light, is eternally, infinitely, and equally present throughout and as His Completeness, His Totality. The universal living Light does not accumulate at any focal point of Its entirety, nor does It ever diminish.

So we can perceive that there is nothing that really accumulates at all, in and as this boundless ocean of ever-living Light.

Another important fact to consider is that the water of the eddy never comes to a stop. It is constantly in action. Not one drop of this focal point called an eddy ever becomes inactive. Nor does one drop of this water come to a stop in its ceaseless, circular movement. *All* of the water of the eddy constantly circulates and continues on its way.

Incidentally, all movement, all activity, is circular. Nothing moves in a straight line. The physicists state that there is no such thing as a straight line in nature. It is noteworthy that the circle symbolizes completeness. There is neither beginning nor ending as a circle. It is even said that the ceaseless activity, when referring to the body, is called the "circulatory system."

But our point is that the ceaseless, irresistible, irrepressible activity of the eddy never does come to a stop. The constant flow of the water of the stream itself is the ceaseless flow of the water that is observed in the form of the eddy. I have dwelt quite extensively on the foregoing facts because they are of tremendous importance in our further revelations. Now that these facts are perceived, let us continue with our revelations of the universal ocean of ever-moving, circling, living Light.

As we observe the eddies of a flowing stream, we note that they are seen only at the surface of the water. Then, too, the stream is confined within and as the boundaries of its banks. Here you can see that there are two aspects of this simile that are inadequate and faulty. So let us realize once and for all that the universal ocean of ever-living Light is boundless, immeasurable, and unconfined.

There is another very important fact that we will now discuss. Let us assume that the eddies of the stream are omnipresent in and as the entirety of the stream itself. In this way, we can also realize that this genuine, universal ocean of living Light is entirely composed of eddies. *This last statement, Beloved, is a very good simile.* This is true because, truly, this Universe, Infinitude, God, consists of countless forms of ever living, moving, surging Light—Life—in and as an infinite variety of innumerable Forms.

Consider well this last statement, for it is important to our complete perception of our universal Identity as well as our specific Identity. You see, the eddies, or living Light in Form, *are* the very Substance that is this Universe. But this is not all. The eternal, changeless, irresistible surge and flow of the universal Light is the eternal, changeless, irresistible surge and flow of the entire universal Substance. And it is also the irresistible, eternal, changeless surge and flow that is going on constantly as the activity of all Substance *in Form*.

From the foregoing, you can perceive that there is no separation of the infinite Substance, which is Consciousness. Neither is there a division of the activity of this Substance, which is Consciousness in action, or Omniaction. There simply is no such thing as a separate substance in form with activity of its own, separate from or other than the infinite, irresistible Activity which is this Universe — God — in action.

The infinite, boundless, ever-circling, constantly moving Light is the indivisible Consciousness that you are, that I am, and that everyone is. The simile of the eddy may be compared to the Body right here, or to the focal point of your fulfillment of a specific purpose at the moment. In any event, you can perceive the inseparability of all Substance and all Activity, and this is of the utmost importance.

There are many ways in which this simile may help to clarify and point up certain revelations that have appeared in former writings, classes, and on tape recordings. You will recall that we have spoken of many lights in a room and the fact that the light of each lamp was specifically *that* light and no other, yet the light in the room was one indivisible light.

This simile at least served to point out the indivisible, though specific, Nature of all existence. But never did it present the *universal* activity that is so important if we are to perceive the genuine, omniactive Nature of the Universe. In the simile of the stream being the eddy and the eddy being the stream, we do have a sense not only of the living Light, but we also can perceive the activity that is constantly going on in and *as* this living Light. And the activity is of vital importance for each one of us to understand.

Now we can perceive that the boundless, universal ocean of ever-moving, living Light is the Substance of all Its Forms, and the Form of all Its Substance. As stated before, all movement is circular. The overall movement is boundless, and it is comprised of countless distinct, but not divided, movements. All activity is rhythmic activity. All Substance in Form — and all Substance *is* Form — moves and acts in and as a definite rhythm. In other words, every so-called eddy moves at its own specific rhythm. Yet its movement is not in the least divided from the infinite, rhythmic Omniaction that is the Universe in action. There are infinite rhythms constantly acting as Infinity in perfect, rhythmic activity.

In our book *You Are the Splendor*, it is revealed that everything in existence moves at its own rhythm, so we will not repeat here what has already appeared in print. However, we should mention the word *tempo*. There is a definite tempo for each rhythmic activity. This has to do with that which is called the *speed* of the activity. For instance, the Earth planet orbits around the sun at one definite, perfect, rhythmic tempo, or rate of speed, and it turns on its axis at another tempo. All the while, it is said to be traveling with our galaxy at a terrific rate of speed.

I do not wish to seem intellectual in presenting these facts, which are entirely spiritual facts. We know that all activity is God — conscious, living, loving Mind — in action. But it is necessary to know and to understand just why all activity is specifically *that* activity and no other, yet all activity is essentially the same perfect, indivisible, rhythmic activity.

Let us consider the activity of specific Identities whom we may know. Some Identities move, work, talk, and act very rapidly indeed, while some move, act, and talk at a more deliberate or slower tempo. But this does not mean that they are separate Consciousnesses in action.

The activity of the Body is a case in point. As you know, the breathing goes on at one definite tempo, we walk at another tempo, and the supposed digestive activity takes place at another specific tempo. Also, the supposed beat of the heart is said to have its perfect, rhythmic tempo. There are many other examples we could mention, but I am sure that the foregoing will be sufficient for our present purpose. Suffice it to say that the Earth planet may be compared to one specific eddy, moving in and as at least three undivided rhythmic tempos. This Body right here may be compared to a specific eddy acting in and as numerous rhythmic tempos.

There is nothing existing that can change, obstruct, or interfere with the irrepressible, irresistible orbiting of the planets around the sun. The tempo at which they move cannot be accelerated, nor can it be retarded. The rhythmic tempo of each activity that is going on in and as our Earth planet never changes in the least. And, Beloved, it is important for you to realize that there is nothing existing that can possibly obstruct, change, or interfere with the perfect, ceaseless, rhythmic tempo of *every* activity of this Substance in Form that you call your Body.

Our simile of the infinite Ocean of ever-moving living Light, comprised of countless eddies of this ever-active living Light in Form, should help immensely in your perception of your eternal, perfect, uninterrupted, rhythmic activity. Furthermore, it should reveal how it is, and why it is, that the activity of your daily experience and the activity of your bodily experience is completely inseparable from the infinite, perfect activity which is God in action, or Omniaction.

In this same way, we can perceive that:

No Substance is ever confined within Its Form. Furthermore, the Substance that is the universal Ocean of perfect, eternal Light—Life— cannot be kept out of, or excluded from, the

Substance of the Form Itself. This is true because the universal Substance is the Substance of the Form, and the Substance of the Form is the universal Substance.

In like manner, the activity of any Substance in Form cannot be confined in or to the outline or delineation of the Form. Neither can the universal Activity — Omniaction — be excluded from the activity of the Substance in Form. It is all identically the same activity. There is absolutely nothing about the outline or delineation of the Form that confines the omniactive Substance within the Form; nor is there anything existing as the delineation of the Form, called skin, that excludes the universal, ever-perfect, rhythmic movement from being active within, and as, the bodily activity.

The foregoing revelation is of tremendous importance to those who seem to be faced with some imperfect bodily activity.

For instance, sometimes it is said that the heart beats too rapidly or that its activity is interfered with or obstructed. Then again, it may be that the activity of digestion or the breathing seems to be imperfect or restricted in some way. It also may seem to be obstructed. But the perception of the Truth that the entire Universe — God — is active in, through, and as the *only* activity of the Body reveals clearly the impossibility of any such condition or situation. Then, as this is fully perceived, you will discover that the *perfect*, rhythmic activity, which is Perfection in action, is manifested. Your friends will imagine that you have had a healing, but you will know better. You will know that it is entirely your conscious perception of the unobstructible, omnipotent, irresistible, irrepressible Action that is manifested as It should be, as It has forever been, and as It is.

Let us now consider the activity of your daily Life and experience. Perhaps it seems that something is always interfering with your perfect, purposeful activity. This falsity can appear in many guises. It may seem nothing goes right at the office, in the studio, or in the home. It may appear that your activity as a composer, an artist, or as a performer is literally filled with strain, struggle, frustration, and disappointment. What about your activity as a school teacher, a saleswoman, or a salesman? Does it appear to be fraught with difficulties? Now let us perceive how it is, and why it is, that these illusions concerning activity appear to be evident.

First: *what is the difference between the bodily activity and your activity as you go about your daily affairs?* Where does one aspect of your activity — bodily — leave off and another aspect of your activity — business, home, profession, etc. — begin? Where does the eddy leave off and the water of the river begin? Or where does the water of the river leave off and the water of the eddy begin? *Nowhere.* There is no separation in Omniaction. Why, then, the seeming struggle? Well, it is as though you had gotten out of your rhythm. But this is not all. It is as though you were turned around and were swimming against the tide.

Now let us perceive how it is, and why it is, that you *seem* to be moving against the ever-rhythmic universal activity instead of moving with and *as* this activity. Such a situation as we have just mentioned can only seem to be when you are trying to do something of and by yourself. It is as though you imagined that you were one little separate mortal and that your activity was confined just to you alone or your little separate orbit. Always this is duality, and duality always means struggle and striving. It is necessary for you to clearly perceive that you *are* the indivisible, universal Substance and your activity is the inseparable, universal Activity. You will find that you are not a *do*-er. Rather, you are a *be*-er. Your activity is not something that you do of yourself. Rather, it is something that you *are*.

Does this mean that you just sit with folded hands and remain inactive? Indeed, it does not mean anything of the sort. You will find that you are more active than you have ever known your Self to be. The difference being in the fact that now you know that of yourself you can do nothing, of yourself you can know nothing, and you can have nothing because of yourself you *are* nothing. The only way you can possibly exist is by *being* the universal, indivisible Omnipresence. The only way in which you can act is *as* the inseparable, universal, perfect, effortless, rhythmic Omniaction Itself.

You know, in our *effort* to do something or to be something of ourselves, it is as though we were trying to make God — the Universe — be what God already is. Again, it is as though we were trying to force Omniaction to be omniactive. Of course, this is ridiculous. But our point is that when you realize that the activity in which you are engaged is the universal, ever-perfect Universe in irresistible, unobstructed activity, you discover that you are free of all struggle or strain. It simply takes place, and it goes on so smoothly and so beautifully that you really marvel.

One student told me that he walked around in constant awe at the way all of this glorious activity takes place. This will be your experience too, Beloved, when you not only perceive, but *know*, that you *are* that Truth which you perceive. Then, too, you will realize that your activity is that activity which you know to be universal.

Does all of this sound too good to be true? Well, contemplate these Truths and try it. You will find that it is true — it is Truth and *You are this Truth*.

Oh, there is tremendous power in this way of perception. What is the Power that makes all activity so perfect, so indivisible, and above all, effortless and harmonious? *Love*. Love is the Power. It is Love that is the indivisible Oneness of all Substance in Form. It is Love that is the omnipotent Perfection of all Substance and Its Activity. It is Love that is the

Beauty of the Life that is ever beautiful. So, Beloved, we never leave *Love* out of our contemplation.

For a more complete comprehension of the Universe in action, let us return to Its perfect, rhythmic activity. All of us know that the tides of the ocean are rhythmic. So the movement of the ocean is a rhythmic movement. It is also known that there are tides of the atmosphere and that the land surfaces of the earth move in the same way that the ocean tides move. Just recently, I read a report by experts who have been exploring the uttermost depths of the ocean floor. These experts state that the substance at the bottom of the ocean is in constant movement. Of course, we don't see or feel the movement of the Earth planet. Nonetheless, it is constantly going on.

Actually, we ourselves are in constant movement, even when it seems that we are completely still. We have to move as the Earth planet moves. Thus, we are orbiting around the sun, we are revolving or turning as the earth turns on its axis, and we are, according to all reports, traveling with our galaxy at tremendous speed through the atmosphere toward and into what is called outer space. All of this activity is going on right now, and we don't seem to be aware of it.

Each one of the movements is circular. Each one of them moves at its own rhythm and tempo. In illumination, we experience countless rhythmic activities which it seems we know nothing about, so long as we seem to be limited and bound by a deceptive, concealing cover of illusion. However, it must be said that in full illumination we are aware that we *are* that which we see or experience. We are conscious of *being* all Substance, all activities, all rhythms, and tempos of rhythms simultaneously.

Now we realize that all Substance in Form is the infinite, living Light embodied as Itself. Every galaxy is like an eddy of living Light. You have seen pictures of our galaxy, and no doubt you have noticed that the picture shows our galaxy to be in circular form similar to the eddy we have used as a symbol. We know that the movement of planets around the sun is circular. Pictures of stars and planets show that they also are circular in form, as well as moving in a circular pattern.

There is a scientific book entitled *The Inhabited Universe*, and it is a Premier book, published in paperback form. The authors are Kenneth W. Gatland and Derek D. Dempster. I am confident that it would be helpful if you would read at least certain sections. Of course, I cannot quote verbatim, but I can tell you that these scientists are aware of the boundless Nature of the Universe. They are also aware that all Substance moves in waves, as we have stated, and that even the earth, which seems to be solid matter, really consists of a Substance that is completely nonmaterial. They know that what they call *reality* is not solid density or darkness.

Isn't it wonderful that these dedicated physicists are coming to the conclusion that matter as such does not exist and that the Universe is boundless, ever moving as circular waves of motion? And the most important aspect of all this is the fact that the waves are inseparable. Do the waves separate the water of the ocean? Indeed no. And neither do the waves of universal living Light, surging and flowing in perfect rhythmic movement, separate this Light— Life—which is God.

Oh, if you can only perceive and experience this wonderful "feeling" of *being* this living Light in Its perfect movement, you will know—really know— the sheer ecstasy of joyous, free living.

Years ago, the physicists believed that substance consisted of innumerable lines, which were formed of dots. However, the dots did seem to be separate one from another. Then they decided that these lines of dots were not really separated dots but that they were solid lines. Now they speak of substance as being waves; but they have come to the conclusion that the wave, the line, and the dot all exist as substance. This is very interesting and revealing. The waves do exist; the dots do exist; but they are not separate dots of a material nature.

The waves are waves of living Light. The dots are living Light in Form. They are the innumerable focal points of universal living Light in Form. They are the universal living Light eddying at a specific point. This is why all Substance exists as Form.

There is no such thing as formless substance. But never does the Form separate the universal, living Light into bits and parts of Itself. Never do we forget the eternal, infinite, indivisible Nature of this infinite Universe, which is God.

Why do we dwell so steadily on the Nature of the Universe? Beloved, *knowledge is power*, and our knowledge of the Universe is our knowledge of what we are. Through the study and investigation of every atom and item of his being and body, so-called man has tried throughout the centuries to discover what he is, and, as yet, he still seems to be seeking understanding and knowledge of himself. Starting from a little limited standpoint, he naturally would only arrive at a limited knowledge of his existence. *No*—we must, even as did Dr. Einstein, know and understand what the Universe *is* if we are to know and to understand what we *are*, and because we start from a limitless standpoint—the Universe—our knowledge and understanding can be without limits.

Every galaxy is like an eddy of living Light. Every star, every planet is like an eddy of living Light. This is also true of our Earth planet; and it is true of every blade of grass, every grain of sand. This Body, right here, is like an eddy of the universal living Light. Every so-called cell, atom, or item of this Body is like an eddy. But this is not all. Even as there are innumerable eddies of this ever-active Light, so it is that there are innumerable rhythms of activity, constantly circulating in, through, and as all Substance in Form. This same indivisible activity is constantly circling and circulating in, through, and as the activity of every so-called atom, cell, item, or assumed organ that constitutes this Body right here.

Now you can perceive how it is, and why it is, that *nothing* ever comes to a stop. The Light flows, circulates, and then continuously flows on. This is why there can be no accumulation of Substance. This is why all Substance is ever new; yet, paradoxically, all Substance is the same Substance. This is why the Substance in Form you call this Body could never accumulate one iota of anything. This Body could never experience having, or being, either an excess or a deficiency of any substance.

There is not one iota of this Body that ever comes to a stop. How could there be a complete or even partial stoppage of the constant, omnipotent surge and flow of the omnipresent, universal Light which is all Substance? The activity of this infinite, living Light is Omniaction —*all* activity —equally everywhere.

In most instances, when some disease or abnormalcy seems to be present in and as the body, it is believed to have begun, to have developed, and grown worse. Of course, this would mean that some disease, infection, etc., had either entered the Body and come to a stop at that point or that it had originally developed in or as the body and then had grown progressively worse.

Of course, we are speaking of an illusory substance and activity now, but we are not deceived. In the first place, the Body can no more have anything or be anything of itself than can the eddy of the stream. So no disease germ, infection, etc., could begin in, or as, the Substance of the Body.

Secondly, the entire Essence of this Body is the ever circling, moving, living Light, and It does not come to a stop anywhere or at any moment. There is not a pinpoint in Infinity where this surging, flowing movement is not going on. Neither is there a moment in Eternity — which is now — when this irresistible Omniaction is not present and active.

Beloved, can you see what this means to those who seem to have a sick or diseased body? What we have realized and are perceiving here is Absolute Truth. It is absolutely, undisputedly true, and this Truth does manifest Itself as perfect Substance, perfect Form, and perfect Activity.

So often it is believed that the activity of some aspect of the body is erratic or is imperfect. Perhaps it is assumed to be too fast or too slow. Then again, there may be an illusion that something is obstructing or interfering with the perfect activity of the ever-circling movement of the entire Essence of the Body.

Well, you can perceive that the Body has no activity that is separate from the universal Omniaction. Thus, not one iota of the Body can act or react of Itself. The entire activity of every aspect of the Body has to be as irresistible, as unobstructible, and as perfect as Light in action. It has to be this way because it *is* the universal living Light Itself in action. Suppose it seems that some bodily activity is obstructed. Nothing that is the Body ever comes to a stop. So how could there be *anything* that could accumulate, harden, or act as an obstruction? It can't. It doesn't. Let us never overlook the constancy of the universal Light in Its ceaseless action.

Sometimes it is said that some aspect or element of the body is deficient, (This is mainly the reason why vitamin preparations are in such great demand today.) Well, we have already discussed the fact that there is never a deficiency, nor is there an excess of the universal living Light. We know that there could no more be an excess or a deficiency of this Light in and as the Form than there could be a deficiency or an excess of this Light as the atmosphere, the stars and planets, the galaxies, or of the boundless, universal Substance Itself. So when someone calls for help and tells you that he has some deficiency — of any kind, whether of Substance or of Activity — you will perceive the completeness that is ever-present, and you will also perceive the constant, complete Omniaction which is ever-active. There is never an increase, nor is there a decrease of the complete, boundless, infinite Substance. Neither can there be an increase or a decrease of this Substance in Form.

There is one aspect of an illusory sense of body that seems to be very troublesome, and this fallacious aspect is obesity. Many jokes are concocted about this illusion, but to the one who seems to be enduring it, I can assure you it is not funny at all. Actually, I know of no illusory aspect of the body that is so discouraging and so depressing as is obesity. So, here again, it is necessary to know how it is, and why it is, that there can be no such thing as too much substance, nor is there any extra substance to the normal Body.

If there could be an excess of Substance in or as the Body, the universal, ever-flowing, surging, living Light — all Substance — would have to come to a stop at that focal point. It would have to be immovable in order to accumulate. Furthermore, this false accumulation would have to be held or confined within the outline, form, or delineation of the Body.

We know that there is nothing about the delineation of the Body that confines Its Substance, and we also know that there is nothing about the outline of the Body that keeps out the irresistible, surging, omniactive, universal Substance. So we can perceive that any illusion of obesity *has* to be illusion. It has to be hallucination and nothing else. All movement is free, effortless, and graceful, and the movement of the Body is as beautiful, as free, effortless, and graceful as is the movement of the gently swaying bough of a beautiful tree or the graceful sweep of the wave of the ocean. Let us stop this thing of bowing down to an illusion called obesity.

Of course, there does seem to be the illusion of an excessive appetite for food, but this excess appetite is not what it seems to be. The psychiatrists are misinterpreting it too, but at least they are closer to the facts about this illusion than are the physicists. No one would ever crave food or drink if it were fully perceived that all Substance is eternally and infinitely complete — wanting nothing, needing nothing. Neither would anyone ever yearn for anything at all. When it is recognized that the Identity is eternally, constantly complete, it means the obliteration of any seeming craving or yearning for something that he already *has* and *is*.

You know, there have been many of us who have believed that we yearned for God, too. Yet when we "woke up," or became fully cognizant of our genuine and only Being, we realized that we did not really yearn *for* God. We perceived that always it was God, our only Being, announcing Its Self as our Self. It is like the signal mentioned in the book *You Are the Splendor* — it "rang a bell," signifying that All was well, for God is All, and God is always well and complete. Thus it is with any so-called yearning or craving; it is only an illusion of incompleteness. But actually, it is the Principle, *Completeness Itself*, signifying Its Presence.

One of the most cruel of all hoaxes that has ever been foisted upon assumptive man is the illusion called aging or old age. Make no mistake about it, this illusion can *seem* very real. There appears to be such hopelessness about it because it is falsely considered to be inevitable. There is supposed to be no betterment and no end for it excepting the final illusion called death.

Yet the illusion called old age is no more genuine than is the illusion called youth, nor is it any more true than is the illusion called sickness, disease, pain, or any other abnormal, inharmonious deception about the Body. Anyone who has seemed to experience this miasma and has, through enlightenment, perceived its utter fallacy knows how dreadful it can *appear* to be. So let us discuss this utterly false assumption and realize how it is, and why it is, that such a so-called situation or condition is impossible. With this purpose in view, we will return to our symbol, the eddy.

We have discussed the fact that the Substance of the eddy is constantly *new* and fresh. Although, as we have stated, paradoxically, it is the *same* Substance or Essence, yet it is ever new because entirely new water is constantly circulating as that Substance and flowing on. The Body is like an eddy in and as the infinite ocean of living Light. Its Substance is always new and fresh. This is true because nothing ever comes to a stop at this focal point and because the Substance of this Body is never confined *within* Its outline or Form.

Now, how could this Body age or go through an aging process when It is all new — brand-new — this and every moment? How could It deteriorate, decay, or become decrepit? How could the ever-new Substance of this Body stiffen, harden, or weaken? How could the activity of the omniactive, ever new Substance that is this Body in action ever be any slower or any faster? Oh, Beloved One, none of these illusions is possible. It simply cannot be because it is utterly impossible for any Substance to simultaneously be entirely new and to be aging or old.

One more point is important in this perception. This is the fact that there is no time. Actually, there is no time, as the space physicists know very well indeed, but I hope we can discuss this fact at greater length later on in this book. In any event, we can perceive that the ever new — yet changeless — Nature of the Body precludes the possibility of Its *ever* aging, deteriorating, or being old.

Do you know that despite years of search and research by physicists and medical men, they have been unable to discover why the body ages? They can discover no cause for an aging process. This is not surprising in view of the fact that the Body really does not and cannot age. One day, the physicists may discover why the Body cannot age. Then they will know why It cannot die.

Please know that I am not speaking of a body of matter. *There is no body of matter*. But there is a Body right here, and this Body does not become ill, nor can It ever be or become old and decrepit. Last, but not least, this Body was never born, nor can It die.

111

All of this will be known by everyone when absolute *knowledge* completely dispels all illusion.

In certain aspects of illumination, we do see Forms. The Substance of these Forms is always fresh, new, perfect, and beautiful. But of the greatest importance is the fact that never do we see the form of a baby. It is also true that never do we see an aged body. Always we see the Body as absolutely perfect, beautiful, and at the very peak of Its Perfection. This, Beloved, is the Body we are speaking of here. Actually, there is no other body, and it is futile to even consider a kind of body that does not even exist.

We have now arrived at this question: why does the Body *seem* to deteriorate, age, and die? This tragic miasma seems to continue because so-called man "with breath in his nostrils" has considered this process to be normal, and it has even been called inevitable. Often we hear this deception referred to as a "law of nature." How cruel this would be if it were true. There could be no Love in such a thing as this. *God is Love, so Love is all Substance and all Activity.* In fact, the Totality that is *Love* precludes the possibility of anything troublesome, inharmonious, or tragic.

Yes, throughout the ages, we have been told this fabrication, and being seemingly without knowledge, ignorant, we have blindly believed it. This seeming ignorance is the "absence of mind" we mentioned earlier and which we now realize to be impossible. We know that we are the *Presence of the Mind that is all Knowledge*, and we refuse to accept or to believe any such nonsense.

Jesus certainly made it very clear that whatever we accepted or believed would seem to be our condition or experience. So long as the non-mind—called a born human mind, supposedly functioning in a born brain—believes the fallacies of birth, change, sickness, age, and death, these illusions will seem to be valid. Just this long—and no longer—will they seem to be present and to have power. Furthermore, they will appear to be inevitable.

> A belief must have a believer in order to be a belief. It must have someone to believe it, else it cannot even seem to be a belief.

But the very moment the *I* that I am refuses to accept or to believe a falsity, it can no longer even *seem* to be true or to exist. It makes no difference at all that birth, growth, change, age, sickness, decay, and death have been believed throughout the ages. I do not believe these fallacies. I am not a believer in myths. *I* am the Mind that *knows*. *I* am full, complete Knowledge now. *I* know that *I* am ever new, eternal, and immutable.

The very moment this *I* that I am perceives, acknowledges, and accepts *only* his universal, eternal Being and Body, these fallacies, beliefs of ignorance—non-mind—will no longer even appear in or as his experience, or his Body. But in order to completely refute the phantasmic illusions of the ages, we must know—really know—what we are. Furthermore, we must know why we are what we are, and the knowledge of the "why" has to come as Self-revelation. No one can teach it to you. Self-revelation reveals that it is utterly and completely impossible for us to be separate from, or other than, the eternal, changeless, perfect Being and Body that we are.

Beloved One, this Self-revelation is exactly why you are reading these lines this moment. To know what you are, universally and specifically, means to know *why* you are what you are. This means also that you know you have no choice other than to be what you are because there is nothing else existing that you can possibly be.

Do we have to believe that the Body must become aged, decrepit, and die just because so-called man "with breath in his nostrils" has supinely bowed down to these illusions? Should we consider it impossible that the Body should remain free, perfect, whole, and sound indefinitely? Is anything impossible that is right and good?

Once it was imagined to be impossible to fly. And you know how those without knowledge ridiculed Robert Fulton when he built and launched his steamboat. How they would have jeered at our space flights. It is only because, inherently, we know that all things are possible—no matter how impossible they may appear—that we challenge the limitations and launch into what seems to be the unknown.

Let us be as courageous as are our space engineers and fliers. Let us refuse to be limited by the age-old beliefs that are merely ignorance, or absence of knowledge. Let us challenge these illusions. How? Through *knowledge*. By this I do not mean acquired knowledge, such as that which is, or can be, taught. Rather, I mean the knowledge that cannot be acquired; namely, that knowledge which can only be revealed within and as our own Consciousness. *This knowledge is Power*.

The physicists launch out into fields completely unknown to them and unexplored by them. Are we less intelligent or less courageous than they? Indeed no. In our Bible, we have the promise of eternal Life right here, and this promise is true and valid. Let us at least begin to act on this promise. Let us begin to accept, and to expect, the manifestation of perfect Body, eternally, and of Life eternal right here where we are at this moment. According to our belief, shall it seem to be unto us. According to our knowledge, shall it *really* be, in and as our experience.

You know, medical practitioners will tell you that certain diseases are incurable, but they don't really believe this to be true. If they did, all medical research would be at an end. It is because they do not believe that any disease is completely hopeless and incurable that they keep right on trying to find new means, methods, treatments, etc., as a cure for every so-called disease.

In order to do this, they, too, must launch into new fields. Their experiments sometimes require great courage. Well, we are no less courageous. And we, too, know that there is no illusory disease—no matter how terrible it may seem to be—that cannot be completely obliterated through knowledge. Being the Mind that is all Knowledge is the Power that reveals the manifestation of eternal, immutable, perfect, ever-living Substance and Activity. True it is that our explorations are not in the field of illusory matter. But it is also true that we do not experiment. The Mind that is all Knowledge does not need to experiment. Rather, It remains full open Consciousness, and thus, all the eternal, glorious, infinite Perfection that already *is*, is revealed.

You will note that sometimes I speak of the Universe as being God; sometimes I speak of It as Infinity; and sometimes as just the Universe Itself. I like to return to the word *God* quite frequently because this wonderful word *God* obliterates any hint of intellectuality in my perception. It keeps the "fire" going. It maintains, and sustains the high spiritual Nature of all "seeing" or "Perception."

Words can be quite tricky. They can even appear to be deceptive. Sometimes I have noticed that too many words can seem to dim the magnificent Light that we are. So in our contemplation, it is well to frequently return to the word *God*. Often I just softly, or perhaps inaudibly, say it over and over. And always it brings a great surge of pure *joy*, and oh, such boundless *Love*. There is no danger of "going stale" in our seeing when we keep very close, in and as our Heart, this wonderful word *God*.

Again, it is necessary that we return to our universal Being and Body. And of course, this means a further consideration of our universal Consciousness being our specific Consciousness. It means a further awareness of our universal Substance and Activity being the Substance and Activity that is the Identity —including the Body—that exists right here and now.

We have realized the universal Substance and perceived Its perfect, rhythmic movement. We know now that our Bodies are merely eddies of the universal, rhythmic, omniactive Substance that we are. But now the question arises, "What about the covering, or the Form, of the Body? What makes the outline, the delineation, and Form of this Body? What is the substance of that which is called flesh?" Here again, we shall use the eddy as a simile in order to clarify this puzzling question.

You know that the eddy has form. You know that it has outline, or delineation. What is the substance of the form, or the outline, of the eddy? Isn't this form comprised of the same water that is the substance of the stream? And is not this same substance that is the stream the substance of the eddy? Indeed, the substance of the stream, the substance of the form, or outline, and the substance of the eddy are all one and the same substance.

Nonetheless, we can detect the form of the eddy as a distinct form of the very substance of the water of the stream itself.

You may have noticed that the water at the rim of the eddy is a little more distinct than is the water of the eddy or of the river. It is more as though it were "foamy" or "bubbly." That which makes this distinction of the delineation is the activity of the water. At the rim, or the circumference, of the eddy, the water moves at a rhythmic tempo that is faster than the movement of the stream or of the eddy itself. It is this accelerated rhythmic tempo of the ever-moving water that makes the form of the eddy apparent. But it is noteworthy that this outline, or circumference, does not confine the water *within* the eddy. Neither does it keep the water of the river *out* of the eddy. Rather, the substance of the foam, or outline, the substance of the river, and the substance of the eddy are all the very same substance. It is all the very same water, but it is moving at various tempos.

Thus it is with the Body. That which is called the form, flesh, skin, covering, or whatever, consists of the universal ever-living Light, simply acting or moving at a little different tempo than is the Substance that is outlined, or the universal Substance. But this faster tempo of rhythmic activity does not confine the Substance of the Body within Its outline. Nor does It keep out of the Body the universal living light that is *all* Substance. If the delineation of the

Body—flesh, skin, covering—were to confine the Substance of the Body within Its form or to exclude the universal Substance from Its focal point—the eddy or Body—we would have an existence and a body that was separate from the one infinite, eternal, living, loving, conscious Mind. Furthermore, this universal Life is all that ever lives or is ever alive.

Oh, there is much more pertaining to the Body, but we will go much deeper into this all-important subject in our second volume, the evening class sessions, of this classwork.

Chapter XI

Effortless Living ✓✓

Now let us see how it is that our perception functions when we are aware of *being* the universal, omniactive Light. Let us see how this perception acts in and as our homes, our businesses, our professions, our employment, and our social activities. (Some of us have to forego the latter.)

What is it that makes all of these activities so effortless and so successful? It is our awareness of being what we are. It is our consciousness of *being* the boundless, universal living Light, and it is our awareness of being this Light in perfect, harmonious, effortless action. We live and move and experience being as the very Essence that is this Infinitude. But this is not all. We live and move and have our Being *as* the perfect, rhythmic activity which is Omniaction. It is not that we move *with* the rhythm or *with* the Essence of our universal Being. Rather, it is that we move *as* the Essence and *as* all of Its rhythmic activities. You see, we realize that we *are* the universal Essence and we *are* the universal, rhythmic activities, which we call Omniaction.

This effortless living could never be experienced if we imagined that we, of ourselves, were doing something. As stated before, when we try to *do* or to *be* something of ourselves, it seems that we have somehow gotten out of our rhythm. We seem to function as a rhythm that is unnatural for us. Again, it can appear that our rhythmic tempo is erratic. We can seem to be joyous, free, and successful today, and tomorrow we can appear to be depressed, and it may seem that everything goes wrong. In this case, it may appear that today everything goes easily and smoothly, and tomorrow everything seems to be done with great effort or strain. This could certainly seem to be the case if we were not constantly aware of *being* the universal, perfect, rhythmic Omniaction Itself. Oh, yes, there must be a constancy of this awareness.

But suppose that we are not at all conscious of being this infinite, perfect, rhythmic activity. Well, in this case, it seems that the way grows more difficult all the while and the struggle appears to become greater. And unless we "wake up" and become sincere, unselfed, and dedicated in our study and contemplation, the way just gets too hard, and we get lazy or indolent, or we get discouraged and give up. Then, Beloved, we find that we *seem* to be getting old.

Existence should never be a struggle. The more we seem to struggle the more difficult it appears to be. It is like swimming against the current of a swiftly moving stream. The more we struggle the more resistance we seem to meet. Of course, we know it is possible, apparently, in the so-called human scene, to battle one's way to the top, but at what a cost. And fighting one's way to the top and staying at the top once you get there are two altogether different things.

No! This is not our way. Oh, we are successful all right, but not because we fight or struggle. Rather, we can't help being successful because *we know what we are*, and this knowledge is Power. We are effortlessly successful because we move as the omnipresent, omniactive Light in perfect, rhythmic activity. And above all, never do we attempt to use anyone. Never do we attempt to exert power over anyone. Never do we impose upon or take advantage of anyone. Above all, we are ever ethical and completely honest. Honesty and ethics are Love Itself in action. And we know that *we* are Love in action.

Living as the omniactive, universal, living Light Itself, we find the most wonderful things taking place. Opportunities beyond our fondest dreams just appear, and our entire activity is completely free from struggle. Needless to say, we certainly are free from any frustrating experience. We know nothing of avarice, greed, or mad human ambition. These illusions are not our Consciousness, so they cannot even *seem* to exist in or as our Universe or our daily experience. We never tire; we know nothing of fatigue. Where there is no struggle, there can be no weariness. We find that we are inexhaustible strength. In other words, we "let go." Oh, perhaps we paddle and kick a little just at first, but very soon we find that even this slight effort is unnecessary.

In order to strengthen a foundation for the revelations that are to follow, let us briefly recapitulate some basic Principles of the Ultimate. One point must be constantly clear in and as our Consciousness:

> We are every Truth, every Fact, that we have ever heard or read. We are every Truth that we will ever hear or read. We are every Truth that is or can ever be revealed within and as our own consciousness.

We have spoken of the boundless, universal Light that is all Substance, and we have perceived the indivisibility of this living Light. Now we realize that we are conscious only because we are Consciousness Itself. Well, this boundless, inseparable, omniactive, universal, living Light is the universal Consciousness. Let us perceive that this universal Consciousness that we are is our universal Body. But this universal, indivisible Consciousness—Body—that we are is also the universal Consciousness that is everyone in existence. *This is why we are all indivisibly One.*

It is exceedingly important that we clearly understand the foregoing statements. You see, it is our awareness that the universal Consciousness that we are is the universal Consciousness that everyone is that reveals our inseparable Oneness—and this infinite awareness is inseparable. This perception is so vitally important because this Absolute Truth is why we can never be separate from anything or anyone who is necessary to our complete, successful fulfillment of our purpose in being.

But even as our inseparability is essential to the fulfillment of our purpose, so it is that our conscious Oneness is necessary to the complete fulfillment of purpose of everyone who exists in or as our experience. A shorter way to say it would be: any Identity necessary to our fulfillment of purpose is already present as our Consciousness, and we are already present in and *as* the Consciousness of anyone and everyone to whom we are necessary for his successful fulfillment of purpose. This is why there can be no separation between the right employer and the right employee; no separation between the salesman or saleswoman and the customer; no separation between the friends that are right at the moment; no separation between *any* Identities that are essential to a complete, successful fulfillment of purpose.

Now we realize that we are the infinite, boundless, surging, flowing, ever-active Universe. We also perceive that we are this *specific* Identity and we are this *specific* Body right here and now. We know our indivisible Nature. We know how it is, and why it is, that we cannot avoid being that which we are. Again, we know that we are this boundless, omnipotent, omnipresent, surging, flowing, ever-active Universe. But we also know that this Body right here and now is but a pinpoint of the universal Body, or Consciousness, that we are. We are the perfect, rhythmic activity and all of its rhythmic tempos. We are the irresistible, irrepressible Body of Light, and we are this infinite Body, both universally and specifically. Now, Beloved, we can say, "I am That, and That *I* is the *I* that I am."

And now, in humility, calm, and boundless joy, let us say:

I am eternal, infinite, constant Life being eternally, infinitely, constantly alive. I am eternal, infinite Consciousness being eternally, constantly, infinitely conscious. I am eternal, infinite, constant Love being eternally, infinitely, constantly loving.

There is one Body and one Spirit, which are God's. God is the *I* that I am. God is the Body that I am. I am the Body that God is. There is one universal Body, and I am that Body. There is one infinite, boundless Spirit, Consciousness, and I am that Consciousness. All there is of the *I* that I am is this universal, conscious, living, loving Mind that I am, and this is the universal Body that I am.

All that I am conscious of being as my universal Body, or as the universal Body that I am, I am conscious of being as the specific Body that I am. The perfect, rhythmic Omniaction that I am conscious of being as the universal Body I am is the perfect, rhythmic Omniaction that I am conscious of being as the specific Body that I am.

Only that which I know universally can I know specifically. Only that which I know my Self to be universally can I know my Self to be specifically.

Beloved, you can say all of this Truth in honesty and in great humility. And oh, so much more you can say. As full open Consciousness, you will find there is no limit to the Self-revelation that will surge and flow, and these revelations will be ever greater and more glorious.

Chapter XII

There Is neither Time nor Space

The space scientists will tell you that there is neither time nor space. And they are right. However, there is Eternity and there is Infinity. This is true because Eternity is always *now*, and Infinity is always *here*. In other words, All is *now*, All is *here*. Let us perceive just how it is, and why it is, that these statements are presentations of Absolute Truth.

Being Omnipresent Consciousness Itself, you may suddenly find that you are anywhere in this Universe. You do not project your Self in order to be wherever you find your Self to be. You do not leave the Body and travel through so-called space at a terrific rate of speed in order to be wherever you discover your Self to be.

You do not choose to be at any given point. You do not even decide to be at any specific focal point or area. It is just an instantaneous awareness of being at some specific focal point in the Universe. It is as though without any decision, choice, or voluntary effort on your part, you suddenly find that your complete attention is focused at some specific focal point of your Infinite Consciousness.

How can this be? It is for this reason: before you were actively, consciously aware of being at this point, you were already there. This is true because you are omnipresent. You are constantly everywhere.

You are Omnipresence; thus, you are constantly omnipresent.

You are everywhere because you are *the* Everywhere. But no matter where you find your attention focused, that particular focal point is "here" as far as you are concerned.

For instance, I am here in Vista right now. Suddenly, within the next moment, I may find that I am in New York, China, or Australia. I may even find that I am in what they call outer space or on Mars. But no matter where I am aware of being, that is *here* as far as I am concerned at the moment. I might, if I were on the moon, see the Earth planet as a tiny pinpoint of light. If I didn't know better, the earth would be "there" to me. But of course, I would realize that there is no "there." If I were not aware of this fact, I would not be aware of being on the moon in the first place.

So-called space is supposedly measured by the distance between objects. But when you know there are no solid objects, how can space be measured? And since all Substance is indivisible and there are no separated substances in form, there is no way to measure space. *There is no space.*

So-called time is supposedly measured by an interim *between* events. But when everything is going on simultaneously, there is no interim between events.

A little later, we will discuss at greater length the fact that every activity is taking place infinitely and constantly. For now, let us just realize that there is no way in which so-called time can be measured. All is here. All is now.

It is important to clearly realize this fact. Why? Because we *seem* to limit ourselves unmercifully by looking forward to a future or looking backward at a past. In metaphysics, we were always hoping that some problem would "work out," but this very hope involved a supposed future time in which some seeming problem would no longer exist. In the Absolute Ultimate, we hold steadfastly to the fact that everything good and perfect is right here, right now.

We know there is Perfection and that Perfection is eternal, ever-present, and every-where. We know that Perfection is a universal Constant. So It is constantly present right here and now. Therefore, there can be no problem here and now that is going to be solved tomorrow or next week. Often, we seem to hold on to an apparent problem by falsely believing that it is being solved, resolved, or healed. Oh, Beloved, don't you see — in this way, you are, or seem to be, holding the seeming problem, lack, illness, etc., in the here and now as your present experience.

It is absolutely necessary for you to perceive the constant, eternal *here and now of Absolute Perfection, Absolute Harmony*. Even though we may *seem* to be aware of sickness, pain, sorrow, lack, or whatever, we must realize the here and the now of Absolute Perfection, peace, and complete harmony. Let us stop this thing of seeming to postpone our completeness, our joy, peace, and ever-present Perfection by deluding ourselves that some aspect of our completeness is missing. Let us always realize that no aspect of our Being, Body, or experience is ever going to *become* better or more perfect than it is right here and now.

I am convinced that this mistake is due to our acceptance of methods of healing which we accepted in metaphysics. It is amazing how many of us still cling to the fallacy of healing. Just so long as we seem to believe in healing, we are going to appear in need of healing. Why? Because we are still focusing our attention upon, or at least believing in, present imperfection in one way or another. This mistake would, if it could, make imperfection constant and eternal.

Chapter XIII

Truth, a Universal Existent

Every Truth, or Fact, is a Universal Truth, a Universal Fact. There is nothing true, or a fact, right here and now that is not a fact, or true, everywhere, infinitely and eternally.

There are no temporary facts or truths. Every Fact, everything that is true, here and now, is an eternal Fact, or Truth. Every Fact that is true right here and now is a constant Fact, or Truth. This means that every Fact is constantly, eternally true.

Always be aware that every Truth is an eternally *established* Fact. Every Truth, or Fact, is an omnipresent Truth, or Fact. We have heard and read the statement, "Ye shall know the truth, and the truth shall make you free." Well, we certainly are sure that to know anything is to be that which we know. To know the Truth is to *be* the Truth. We know what we are, and we are what we know. Thus, we *are* the Truth, and our awareness of this Fact makes us free. We could not avoid being free because we are the Truth that is complete freedom. Jesus said, "I am the truth." He didn't say, "I know the truth." But since he could say, "I am the truth," he certainly was aware that he knew the Truth. Knowing and being are the same thing. Being and knowing are the same thing.

If there were no Truth, there would be no Universe. Truth is a universal Constant. If there were no Truth, there would be no you or me. Why? We can only exist because we are the Truth, or Fact, of Existence. This Universe consists of the sum total, the aggregate, of all Truth. But this is not all. Everything and everyone consists of the sum total of all Truth. Even the so-called atom is the aggregate of every Truth. Every cell of the Body, every grain of sand, everything in Form is the sum total of all Truth.

When we say, "I am the Truth," we mean that we are *all* that is true. Being all that is true, it is impossible for us to be anything that is not true. We do not mean that we are part of the Truth or just some of that which is true, We really should realize all that we mean when we say, "I am the Truth." And we should frequently make this statement, "I am the Truth," consciously knowing what we mean and all that we mean.

Now, let us perceive at least some of what we mean when we say, "I am the Truth." For one thing, Truth is omnipresent, omniactive, and omniscient. Thus, we are saying:

I am everywhere present; I am everywhere active, and I am the only activity. I am the all-knowing, omnipresent Mind. I am all knowledge; I am the sum total of all knowledge.

Actually, this is why we can know anything that is necessary for us to know at any moment.

Let us consider another Truth in the aggregate of all Truth. Life is a Fact. Life is Truth. You are alive. Only Life is alive. You are Life being alive. You are the Truth that is Life and the Life that is Truth. You are the Truth that is eternal, constant Life. In order to be alive, you have to be this omnipresent, eternal Life, for this is the only Life there is. Thus, when you say, "I am the Truth," you are saying:

I am birthless, deathless, beginningless, endless, constant, ever-present Life, right here and now.

If some illusion seemed to be a threat against your Life, it wouldn't get very far if you realized this Truth and that you *are* this Truth.

All Truth is Absolute Truth. This means that all that is true, or a fact, is completely perfect. Webster's Dictionary defines the word *Absolute* as "free from imperfection." Perfection is a Fact. It is an omnipresent, eternal, constant Truth. When you say, "I am the Truth," you are really saying, "I am eternally perfect, constantly perfect, and completely perfect, for I am Absolute Perfection."

Consciousness is Absolute Truth. Consciousness is awareness. It is conscious, or aware, of being the Perfection that It is. It is conscious of being the constant, perfect, living Substance that It is. It cannot be conscious of anything that It is not.

You are conscious. You are conscious of being what you are, and you cannot be aware of being anything that you are not. You are the Truth that is absolute, perfect Consciousness, aware of being perfect. When you say, "I am the Truth," you are saying:

> I am consciously perfect. I am conscious Perfection. I am eternal, constant, perfect Substance. I am conscious of being the eternal, perfect, living Substance that I am.

Oh, there are countless Truths that you are. For instance, Omniaction is a Fact, or Truth. Omniaction is Intelligence in action. It is perfect, living, conscious Mind, acting perfectly. It is universal, eternal, and constant. When you say, "I am the Truth," you have really said, "I am Omniaction. I cannot make a mistake or act imperfectly, for I am Mind, Intelligence, acting perfectly and intelligently."

Joy is a universal Truth. Joy is omnipresent, constant, and eternal. Peace is a universal Truth, and certain it is that Completeness is a universal Truth. This is a peaceful Universe. It is a joyous and complete Universe. And only that which is Truth, or a Fact, can be this Universe. You are the Truths that are Joy, Peace, and *Completeness*.

Supply is a universal Truth. Being Completeness, this Universe has to be constantly and eternally complete. But the Supply that *is* this Universe does not come from any so-called outside source. (This is also true of the Supply that *you* are.) There is no outside, so there can be no outside source from which Supply can come. The Universe is Its own Supply. In this same way, the Consciousness that you are is Its own

Supply. Yes, you are the universal, constant, eternal Truth that *is* Supply.

Love is a universal, constant, omnipresent, eternal Truth, and *you are this Truth that is Love.* Love is never temporary. It is never imperfect. Love is Absolute Perfection. You are the true, universal, constant Love that is forever unselfed and true.

Fulfillment of purpose is a universal Truth. This is a purposeful Universe, and this Universe is fulfilling Its purpose equally everywhere and eternally. You are this Truth. You are all the Facts that *are.*

Now, in full knowledge of what it means to say, "I am the Truth," you may be impelled to say:

> I am every universal Truth. The universal Truth I am is equally and eternally present everywhere. I am all Truth, universally and specifically.

It matters not what so-called problem may *appear* on your horizon. You, right here and now, are the Truth that is true in contradistinction to the problem. You do not *have* a problem. In order to have a problem, you would have to *be* the problem. You are not a problem, for you are the Truth, or the true answer. The answer is the Fact that *is*, and you are this Fact. Really, the Truth that is the ever-present answer to every seeming problem is here and now.

Sometimes the question is asked, "Why does one ever seem to have a problem?" The answer is: "Because there is the Truth, or Fact, already established." If there were no Truth, there could be no mistake *about* the

Truth. If there were no answer to a question, the question would never be asked. The Truth, or Fact, of anything has to exist before a question about this Truth could be asked. No one asks a question about nothing. Unless that which is right exists, which occasions a mistake, no seeming mistake can appear to happen. Not even a little child would ask a question of his parent unless he knew there had to be an answer. No. Where is the answer? Right where the question seems to be. Where is the Truth? Right where the mistake about that which is true seems to be.

The question of itself is nothing. It implies ignorance, absence of knowledge, of that which the question is about. The answer is present and is power. That which is present is power. That which is not present is not power. The Truth is present; thus, that which is true, or a fact, is power. A seeming problem, or lack of knowledge of that which is true, is not present; thus, the so-called problem is not power.

You are the sum total of every Truth. This means that *you* are the answer to every seeming problem. You cannot simultaneously be the problem *and* the answer to the problem. As stated before, you cannot *have* anything. Why? Because you *are* everything that is genuine, true, or a fact. This means that you cannot have a problem because a so-called problem is not Truth, or an existing Fact. You are the Truth and you are not the problem. You are the complete answer to every seeming problem. This is why you cannot have a problem.

This Universe is complete as Itself. This is Truth. This Universe is eternally immutable. This is Truth. Being complete, there is never a lack or an absence of anything that is necessary to Its Completeness. Suppose it *appears* that there is a lack or some so-called deficiency in your experience or in your Body. What is the Fact, the Truth, in contradistinction to this mistake? *You are.* Why? Because *you are the Truth.* You are that Truth that is Completeness. In the entirety of this Universe, there is nothing that is necessary to Its Completeness that can be missing or absent. Instead of a deficiency, there is constantly a sufficiency. Because this Universe is immutable, there is never anything added to or taken from the changeless Completeness that *is* this Universe. Remember now:

> You are this Universe. What this Universe is, you are, and nothing else.

Because this Universe is immutably complete, there is never anything missing or absent from Its Completeness. Neither is there ever anything added to Its changeless Completeness. There is never an excess, nor is there a deficiency, nothing missing, and only that which is necessary to Completeness exists. When we say, "I am the sum total of all Truth," we are really saying:

> I am the Principle, Completeness, Itself. I am more than complete; I am the Truth that is Completeness. I am the Truth that is the answer to any illusion that there is an excess or a deficiency.

Chapter XIV ✓

The Constancy of Consciousness

The word *Consciousness* is of tremendous importance in our spiritual vocabulary. Many students of the Absolute consider this word to be the most important of all words. There is no doubt but that a complete awareness of its meaning is of vital importance to all of us.

Consciousness is awareness. Consciousness is an *ever-present* awareness. Consciousness is now. Consciousness is here. Neither so-called time nor space is involved in the word *Consciousness*. Consciousness always means that which is here and that which is now. When you say, "I am," the very word *am* means here and now. You would not say, "I am over there." You would not say, "I am yesterday," or, "I am tomorrow." No. Just to say, "I am" really means that you are conscious of *being* right here and right now.

There is another word that is of greater importance than most of us have realized. This word is *constancy*. Let us perceive why this word is of such great importance in our spiritual vocabulary. All of us have seemed to have the following experience. As we have studied and contemplated in the early morning, we have been greatly enlightened, and we are very aware that the Truth is true. Then it seems necessary for most of us to go on about our daily affairs, which do seem to take us into a world of appearance. Before long, it is as though we had never studied or contemplated that morning at all.

The appearance of imperfection, inharmony, etc., seem to crowd upon us, and before we know it, the Truth seems to be forgotten and the world of appearance seems to be all that is true or real.

There is another aspect of this seeming absence of constancy in and as our experience. Perhaps we are quite calm, peaceful, and assured that Truth is true. We may even be inspired and somewhat illumined. Then suddenly something unexpected will appear that seems very serious, or perhaps a crisis of some sort seems imminent. Often when something like this seems to happen, Truth will be temporarily forgotten, and fear or doubt will seem to hold sway.

Oh, all of us have seemed to have these experiences. Now, let us perceive what is to be seen—during our contemplation—that will mean a continuous, steady, constant awareness of that which is true. And this awareness of Truth will remain, no matter what seems to go on during our daily affairs.

Let us not be caught unaware. Let us not wait until the world of appearance seems to bear down upon us or to suddenly appear as something shocking. During our contemplation, let us consciously perceive, very definitely, the constancy of Consciousness. Constancy is an Absolute Truth. One of the definitions found in Webster's Dictionary for *constancy* is "truth."

And he defines the noun *constant* as being "invariable. Not subject to change." Indeed, it is true: Constancy is a universal, immutable, eternal, omnipresent, constant Truth.

It would be well, if, during our contemplation, we would be aware of the universal, eternal, omnipresent, constant Nature of *every* Truth. This means to be conscious of the eternal, uninterrupted Presence of the sum total of all Truth, or all that is true. But it means more than this. It means to be aware of the *immutable* Nature of constant Consciousness. Constancy never fluctuates; It never ebbs and flows; It never comes and goes; It is never more nor less. It is a constant, changeless, eternal, ever-present Absolute Truth, *and you are this Truth*. Constant Consciousness—and you are constantly conscious—is conscious Constancy. Conversely, conscious Constancy is constant Consciousness.

The fact that we go about our daily affairs does not mean that the Truth that is conscious Constancy becomes absent. Neither does it mean that constant Consciousness—the Consciousness that you are—fluctuates; nor is It interrupted. Always you are completely conscious. Always you are the *same* Consciousness. Always you are conscious, so always you are constantly conscious.

And so, Beloved, your very Existence is the ever-present, eternal Truth that is constant Consciousness. Yes, this moment and always, you are conscious Constancy. Consider these facts during your contemplation, and you will find that they are manifested in and as your daily affairs, your Life, and as your bodily affairs.

Chapter XV

One Body, One Consciousness

One of the most difficult fallacies we have to banish is that this body does seem to be a separate substance in form. This is not surprising because it does appear that this body consists of a substance of greater density than is the atmosphere, and it does appear that this substance in form is blocked off in an area of space of certain dimensions. But of course, we know that we live and move and have our being in and as a dimensionless Universe. There can be no dimensions where there is no space.

In any event, it is because all Substance is the same Essence that, actually, the Body is not a substance of density at all. It only appears to be a separate body because It appears to be dense or solid and because It seems to be a different substance than is the atmosphere. Then, too, it does add to the seeming misconception about the Body to have It appear to be dimensional.

We simply must come to the point where we are completely through with this mistaken concept of Body. We must begin to perceive that this Body is not a separate, solid substance, blocked off here in certain dimensions. Certain it is that this Body does exist in and *as* Form. But due to the Nature of the

Substance of this Body and the activity of this Substance in Form, we cannot actually refer to It as being dimensional. We have used the simile of the ocean being the eddy and the eddy being the ocean, and this has helped us to realize the inseparability of this Body from the universal Body. Now let us go further in this realization.

The Bible states that there is one Body, and this is true. But it also mentions the fact that there are many members of this one Body. Now, a *member* of the Body is not something separate from, or other than, the Body Itself. The Member of the Body *is* the Body, just as the Body *is* every Member of the Body. As we have stated before, the universal Consciousness you are is the universal Body you are, and this Body here is but a focal point of the universal Body that you are.

Now, let us consider the fact that this focal point of your universal Body is a *Member* of your universal Body. You would never say that any Member of this body was something separate from, or other than, this Body Itself. You would not even imagine that the so-called heart was something separate from this Body; neither would you be convinced that it was comprised of a substance or activity that was something other than this Body. You know that this Body *is* the Substance and the Activity of that which is called the heart; you also know that the aspect of this Body called the heart is the Substance and the Activity that *is* this Body.

143

Now, let us consider this fact from the universal, as well as the specific, standpoint. The universal Consciousness that you are *is* the universal Body that you are. The specific Body that you are, at this focal point, is a member of the universal Body that you are. This Body right here, being a *member* of the universal Body you are, is not something separate from, or other than, the universal Body you are.

In like manner, the universal Body you are is not something separate from, or other than, this member of your universal Body. The Substance and Activity of the universal Body that you are *is* the Substance and Activity of this Body, for *this* Body is a member of the universal Body that you are. The Substance and Activity of this member of the universal Body you are *is* the Substance and the Activity of the universal Body you are. And of course, all of this is Consciousness, and it is Consciousness in action. It is the universal, ever-living Body of Light being this Body of Light right here and now. But it is this Body of Light being the universal Body of Light.

Not one member of this Body moves unless this entire Body is involved. Not one member of the universal Body moves unless the universal Body is involved. If this Body, or even one member of this Body, were to be or to become ill, diseased, inactive, or imperfect, this inharmony, or seeming imperfection, would involve the entire universal Body. If this Body could be subject to imperfection, the universal Body would be subject to imperfection. If this Body were subject to birth and death, beginning and ending, the universal Body would have to be subject to birth and death, or beginning and ending.

It would have to be this way because the universal Body *is* this Body, and this Body *is* the universal Body. I cannot tell you in words how many wonderful things have taken place through the realization of the Truths we have just now presented. So consider them well, Beloved, for there is tremendous power in this revelation.

This Universe is a living, moving, breathing, conscious Essence. It lives, moves, breathes, and acts as the living Consciousness that is alive in Form as every member of Its Body. It lives; It is alive as the Life of this living Body right here. It breathes as the breath of this Body right here. It is conscious as the Consciousness that is this Body right here.

The Life that is alive as this Body is necessary to the Life of each member of this Body. But the Life of each member of this Body is necessary to the Life of this Body. The Life that is the universal Body is necessary to the Life of each of Its members. (And this Body is one of Its members.) The Life of each member of the universal Body is necessary to the Life that is alive as the universal Body.

Now you can see just why Life is eternal. It is the universal Body that lives, moves, breathes, and has Its Being as this Body. This is why this Body could not breathe one breath of Itself or by Itself separate and apart from, or other than, the ever-breathing universal Body. This Body, being a member of the universal Body, has to live, move, and breathe eternally, for the universal, boundless Body is *All*, and It is eternally alive.

It is truly wonderful to realize that the Life that is alive right here and now is the Life that is the everlasting, living Universe. All seeming anxiety about this Body dissolves in the awareness that the Substance in Form that is this Body right here is the eternal, immutable, perfect Substance that is the indestructible, imperishable, eternal, universal Substance Itself—and, Beloved, It is all *You*. It is the universal, living, loving, intelligent Consciousness that you are. Universally, as well as specifically, it is *You*. It is the *I* that I am. It is the *I* that Everyone is. Even though one may appear to be ignorant of this fact, the unalterable Truth remains. There is one inseparable, universal, eternal, perfect, omniactive Body, and all of Us are this Body.

It is the universal Body that is alive as every member of Itself. It is the universal Body that breathes as the breath of every member of Itself. Nothing exists that is the Substance of the universal Body, or any of Its members, that is not a normal, purposeful, perfect member of this universal Body. The member is the universal Body; the universal Body is the member.

> There is one Body and one Consciousness that is this Body—and this Body is the universal Consciousness that you are.

Chapter XVI

The Complete Fallacy of Illusion

We have perceived many Absolute Truths through the revelations thus far presented in this book of classwork. Now it seems necessary to diverge briefly and to speak of that which really does not exist.

All there is as an illusion of man, who is supposed to be born, is an accumulation of so-called human beliefs. In this book, we have touched on this subject, but now it is necessary to go further with this subject.

Man "with breath in his nostrils" consists entirely of this accumulation of human beliefs. These illusory beliefs have not only accumulated throughout the ages, they have also been increasing as every single false belief was added to the former mass of illusion. Whenever one more illusory belief is added to those which apparently have been accumulated throughout the ages, the seeming burden of fear and limitation is just that much more burdensome.

We *must* completely stop this thing of believing any illusory belief that has been bequeathed to us — thus, fastened upon us throughout the ages. We must even refuse to believe any so-called discoveries of the physicists, so long as they imagined that they were only investigating matter. And we must resolutely refute the discoveries of the medical profession, even though, from the strictly human standpoint, they have been remarkable and have helped many who seemed to need them. Nonetheless, they are not for us. Why? Because they are based on the illusion that Substance is born, must change, age, and die. They are based on the illusion that Substance is temporal and material.

Our entire basis is the fact that all Substance is God, and God is all Substance. God is not temporal. God is never born, nor is God subject to death. God is completely Spirit, Consciousness, and thus, the Substance that we perceive is entirely non-material. Incidentally, we have no quarrel and no conflict with the medical profession. We never advise anyone against having medical attention, if this is what seems right to him at the moment. Nonetheless, the Absolute Ultimate recognizes no sick or ailing substance, nor does it try to heal a kind of substance that does not actually exist.

Centuries ago, it was believed that our Earth planet was located right in the center of the Universe. But of course, subsequent discoveries have revealed that our earth is merely one little pinpoint and is not even located in the center of the solar System. Galileo was persecuted because he refused to believe the accepted and accumulated beliefs that had been accepted throughout the ages. And of course, if we speak publicly of the fact that we do not accept any illusory human belief, we are suspect and certainly will be ridiculed. We just keep quiet. We don't have to *say* a thing is true or is not true just because we are convinced of its truth or untruth. It is enough for us just to know what we know and let it go at that. Nonetheless, the accumulated beliefs, even convictions, of the centuries never by one iota changed the position or the location of our Earth planet. It remained and still remains exactly where it has always been.

Of course, we do not mean that we reject anything and everything that has ever been believed just because it has been accepted. Rather, we keep our Consciousness unlimited and open, refusing to believe that anything has to be irrevocably true just because it has been considered to be so. We question, "How do I know this is true? Isn't it possible that subsequent revelations and events may prove that it is a mistaken belief?" In this way only can we dissolve the seeming bonds of accumulated so-called human beliefs.

Today we seem to be embroiled in a conflict of warlike men throughout the world. It has been said that always there have been wars and always there will be wars. But is this true? Indeed, it is not true. Isaiah, the great spiritual Light, did not believe that was inevitable.

> And he shall judge among the nations, and shall rebuke many people: and they shall beat their swords into plowshares, and their spears into pruning hooks: nation shall not lift up sword against nation, neither shall they learn war anymore (Isa. 2:4).

Actually, Isaiah was perceiving rather than prophesying. He was experiencing the revelation that war is entirely the illusion of ages of accumulated beliefs of hatred, fear, and strife and that actually, *this* right here *is* the Kingdom—Consciousness—of God, in which war is unknown.

War is not really a conflict between nations or within nations and ideologies. Basically, if war existed at all, it would be a conflict between that which is true and that which is not true. Peace must, of necessity, be the experience of the Identity himself or herself. So long as the Identity will seem to be in conflict with himself, the illusion of war or conflict will seem to continue. Once peace is discovered to be an eternal, constant Existent and to be the Consciousness of each and every Identity, there will no longer be even an appearance of war.

We must discover peace within and *as* our own Consciousness. We must also perceive that the peace we know and experience is as boundless as is our Consciousness. In contemplation, it is well to perceive the universal Nature of all Consciousness and that our awareness of *being* peace is being revealed within and as the Consciousness of anyone who is an open Consciousness anywhere in the world. This is our way of being actively helpful as far as this apparent world strife is concerned. We will consciously experience the peace that *is* when we clearly perceive that there are not two existences, but One alone.

Fascism, communism, and capitalism are all failures because these ideologies are government by so-called man "with breath in his nostrils." These so-called leaders of nations themselves are but an accumulation of ages of assorted beliefs. Actually, all government must be, and *is*, Self-government. Lao Tse has said, "He governs best who governs least." And he was right. It does seem strange indeed that so-called men should set up leaders and then permit themselves to be blind followers of the blind. The entire history of the world of appearance is proof that this is a fallacious practice. (Incidentally, this is one reason why I am so insistent upon leaving every student completely free and why I refuse to assume the role of leadership.) Even Moses, great as he was, considered himself to be a leader — and he didn't do too well, either.

Oddly enough, there are many sincere students of Truth, or believers in God in a more orthodox way, who feel that they must have a leader. They are very sure that some leader, teacher, guru, master, author, pope, priest, or minister has learned all the answers and that these answers can only be learned through obedience to these leaders. In the Ultimate, there can be no leaders. Our basic premise is that each Identity is complete, whole, all-knowing, all-acting, infinite Being and that he or she is his own revelation and his own revelator. Furthermore, we know that each Identity is his own governor and his own government.

We are never going to realize and evidence complete freedom until we end this delusion that there must be leaders. All of this nonsense is based in dualism. It has its roots in the illusion that all knowledge has been handed down through separate individuals *by* separate individuals. And of course, it is supposed to be such ancient knowledge that it is accepted as gospel truth.

Knowing the background of these illusions, we challenge, or at least question, everything that has been believed for generations. It makes no difference whether these pseudo beliefs are political, medical, or social; they are simply accepted beliefs that have accumulated throughout the ages.

We have been taught that we were born and that we must die. How do we know this to be true? One might say that it has to be true because it has been the experience of every Identity who has ever existed. How do we know that it has to be the experience of everyone? Really, there are some of us who know that it is not genuinely the experience of *anyone*. But even in the illusory human sense of things, are we sure that birth and death are inevitable, illusory experiences?

Let us consider this question quite extensively. We have been taught that certain bodily conditions are fatal or that they are crippling or incurable. Again and again, we have seen proof that this so-called knowledge is faulty. We have been assured that boiling water, steam, or excess heat, in contact with the body, causes pain, burns, and blisters. But we do not take them seriously; too many of us have actually seen the instantaneous refutation of these accepted beliefs. We know better.

We know that once upon a time there was the myth that tomatoes were poisonous, and we have read that certain individuals who accepted this fallacy did seem to die after eating them. But oddly enough, tomatoes are freely eaten today. Yes, and we have seen the evidence that *no* food can be or become destructive to Life. We have seen what is called ptomaine poisoning simply dissolve within what would be called one-half hour.

Oh, we could go on ad infinitum with the proofs we have seen which absolutely refuted the accepted accumulated illusions of a seemingly destructive substance or activity. Oh, yes, we have been told that so-called healing takes time, and we know there is no time, nor is there any such thing as healing. It is said that it takes time and struggle to attain wealth or success. But we've seen that supply and success are not something that have to be attained through long periods of time and struggle.

These perfectly normal existents are already here, within and as the Consciousness of each Identity, and it does not take non-existent time for that which already exists to be manifested. Every experience of sudden success and every instantaneous so-called healing prove that there is no time.

Beloved, you will realize that the title of this chapter is "The Complete Fallacy of Illusion." And of course, illusion is just what we have been discussing. You are not deceived. You know that this dualistic discourse has only been presented because it is necessary for us to be alert to the seemingly entrenched, accumulated beliefs — without a believer — that have appeared to limit and bind so many of us. Now we are alert. Now when any seemingly harmful or limiting illusion presents itself, we can ask, "Is this an eternal Truth, or Fact? Did it begin? If so, wouldn't it have to come to an end?"

We know that anything that is not eternal is not Truth. Thus, it is not a fact. Any seeming presence that is not constant is not true or a fact. Truth is never interrupted. There are no absences in the Presence that is constant, eternal Omnipresence. Right here, the word *Consciousness* is exceedingly important. We may ask, "Am I really conscious of this appearance as a fact? Or am I merely accepting an illusory nothing that appears as an accumulated mass belief? The conscious Mind that I am does not believe. It knows, and It *knows* that it knows."

Sometimes when some illusion seems to be very tenacious and very real, it helps to ask, "Is this a universal mass belief? Is it believed by all the Identities on all the planets? Or is it merely believed by the majority of those who are supposed to be confined to this Earth planet?"

Why should we question in this way? Well, for one thing, it brings about a larger and more impersonal perspective. Even though we are questioning the authenticity of an illusion, it helps to "enlarge the borders of our tent." Perhaps you would feel more comfortable if you were to consider our own Earth planet. If so, that is the way for you.

Suppose that one of our loved ones is all prepared to depart this life because he has lived out his allotted time of "three score years and ten." Oh, there are many, even now, who still seem to be deluded by this myth. But it is known to be an actual fact that many Identities are, even humanly speaking, well over the one-hundred-year mark. And in India there are those who are known to have been visible for hundreds of years. If there were a mass illusory accumulation of belief that so-called man's life should be seven hundred years instead of seventy years, we could certainly see many Identities — even in the illusory scene — who imagined that they were at least seven hundred years old.

For that matter, who is sure that on Mars, on Venus, or on some other planet of our galaxy, the so-called life span may not be considered to be, say, hundreds or even thousands of years. Better even than that would be the knowledge that it is recognized and evidenced on some planets that Life is beginning-less, changeless, endless — even as the *only* Life in existence really forever is.

Not long ago, it was the accepted custom for those who seemed to be ill to be bled with leeches. There will come a day when all the food theories, pills, shots, operations, and the like will be considered to be just as primitive and ignorant as we now consider the bleeding by leeches.

All so-called beliefs change. But Truth does not change. Anything that seems to be subject to change is not Truth; thus, it is not a fact, and we are not governed by it, nor are we in bondage to it.

As stated before, it is not wisdom to dwell too much on this subject of illusion because, after all, we are really talking about something that does not exist. Yet because illusion, with all its accumulated and accepted beliefs, has been so generally accepted, it seems to be wisdom to raise our sights here and perceive that these accumulated beliefs are really just beliefs and *nothing else*—and we don't have to believe them or to be influenced by them.

Chapter XVII

The Fallacy of Comparisons

Now let us speak of the *things that are*. Let us speak of the indestructibility of the Substance that *is*. Let us speak of Its imperishable Nature.

It is not difficult to realize that Mind cannot be destroyed or that Consciousness or Life cannot perish. Well, Mind *is* Substance. Mind is conscious and Mind is alive. Mind, consciously alive, is Substance. This eternal, living Substance is indestructible and imperishable, and this indestructible, imperishable Substance is the Substance in Form that is the Body right here, now and forever.

The fact that this Body is distinctly *this* Body, and no other, does not mean that Its Substance is divided from, or other than, all Substance. We now understand this fact. But let us perceive that all sickness, trouble, lack, etc., are based entirely on illusory duality. It is illusion that makes it appear we have something, as a separate person, that Mary Smith or John Jones does not have. It is also the illusion of separateness that makes it appear that John Jones or Mary Smith has something that we do not have and just might like to have.

How often we have noticed that the desire to have the success, the money, or the social position of someone else seems to arouse self-pity, jealousy, or envy. Oh, all of this is such a deluded sense of the indivisible Oneness of all-living, conscious, loving Mind. No identity can have something that is not the Substance, the Activity, and the experience of every Identity. Actually, no one can really *have* anything. This is true because every Identity *is* All. This means that every Identity is the very Consciousness that comprises the Substance and the Activity of everything he could possibly seem to want or to need.

The Omnipresence that *is*, is equally present everywhere and eternally. The Omnipresence that *is*, is equally present in and as every Identity in existence. Nonetheless, this illusion of inequality or partiality — duality — continues to seem to be in evidence, and this illusion always leads to comparison.

It is surprising how often we indulge in the duality of comparison. We compare our so-called health, happiness, wealth, success, etc., with that of someone we falsely consider to be another, or separate, person. We may imagine that this so-called person has more money, health, wealth, happiness than we have. We may wish that we had as much understanding of Truth as some seemingly more fortunate person has. Then, too, we may feel that we have more of something good or desirable than has the man next door. It has been said that comparisons are odious. But actually, comparisons are basically false. In and as the inseparable Oneness that we are, there can be no comparison. The word *comparison* implies otherness, duality, separateness. Let us be very alert to this fallacy.

You can see that we are just pointing out a few of the pitfalls of duality. We do not make denials about duality and fallacies. Rather, we just realize our inseparable Oneness, which makes comparisons impossible.

Chapter XVIII

To Know Is to Be

Now, here are some statements of Truth that are very powerful and very much worth contemplating at quite some length:

> The Known, the Knowledge, and the Knower are all One and the same. I am that which I know. I am the complete Knowledge, and I am the omnipresent, omniscient One who knows.

Beloved, you are Omniscience, or the Mind that is all knowledge. This Mind that is all knowledge is Substance, and the Substance that It is, does exist in and as Form. It is the Substance of everything you see, perceive, or know. It is the Substance of everything and everyone that exists in or as your experience.

Above all, when It is seen—really seen—by the "eye that is single," It is perceived to be living Light. It is Beauty Itself. It glows. It scintillates. It is obviously ecstatic. In short, It is Light, as Form, being alive. It is Life Itself, being alight. It is constant. It is continuous. It is ageless, timeless, and changeless. It can never disappear, for Life can never depart or disappear from Itself. It does not fluctuate. It does not come, nor does It go. It is never more nor less. It simply *is*; and *You are It*, even as *It is You*.

You are the all-knowing, living, perfect, conscious Mind that is this Body of Light. This Mind that you are is your only Substance. This Mind that you are is the only Form of your Substance. This living Mind that you are is the only Activity going on in or as your omniactive Substance. It is all you know to be you.

Yes, the Mind you are is Light. *You know the Christ-Consciousness that you are.* This knowing is knowledge, and the Mind that knows *is* Knowledge. Knowledge is *Light*, even as ignorance, seeming lack of knowledge, is darkness.

> For God, who commanded the light to shine out of darkness, hath shined in our hearts, to give the light of the knowledge of the glory of God in the face of Christ Jesus (2 Cor. 4:6).

You know that seeming darkness is only ignorance. And you have perceived that ignorance would seem to be an absence of Mind, Intelligence, Knowledge. Of course, you now realize that it is utterly impossible for Mind to be absent because there are no vacuums in the Omnipresence which *is* Mind.

What is it that makes the Substance in Form called the Body appear to be dark, dense, or solid? Why do all so-called material objects appear to be dark or solid? Beloved, it is ignorance. It is only a seeming lack of knowledge of the genuine Nature of the Substance that is here. All there is of that which is called matter is ignorance. This, Beloved, is why the physicists say that matter, as such, is sheer illusion.

Nonetheless, they know that there is something in form here where these seeming material bodies or objects appear to be.

Indeed, there *is* Something in Form right here where there appears to be this body that *seems* to be dense and dark—and that Something is Light. This Substance in Form you call your Body consists of the living, conscious Mind that is all Knowledge. And you will recall that *Knowledge is Light,* even as ignorance is darkness.

> The Body of Light is Light because It is the living Mind that is all Knowledge in Form.

The Presence of this living, conscious, all-knowing Mind precludes the possibility of any presence of ignorance being here as this Substance in Form. So you see that, actually, there is no material body. There is no absence of Mind here. There is no darkness, no density, or solidity here. But there is a Body here, and It is the Body that consists of full and complete Knowledge. And of course, this is the Body of Light. All Substance is intelligent because all Substance is the all-knowing Mind that is Light. There is no non-intelligent substance, for there is no absence of Mind.

There are many statements in our Bible, particularly in the New Testament, that point up the Truths we have just been discussing. Very revealing indeed, are those which follow:

> The light of the body is the eye: if therefore thine eye be single, thy whole body shall be full

of light. But if thine eye be evil, thy whole body shall be full of darkness. If therefore the light that is in thee be darkness, how great is that darkness! (Matt. 6:22-23).

To see—perceive—with the "single eye" means to *know*, or to be Absolute *Knowledge*. Absolute Knowledge is completely free from duality. The Mind that is Absolute Knowledge is single Vision. It sees God and only God. No wonder Jesus said that perceiving as this Knowledge would reveal the Body of Light. But if it appears that we are ignorant, or are not the Presence of the *One and Only All-Knowing Mind*, it certainly will appear that this Body consists of darkness, density, solidity.

Jesus states that the Light is already in you. Actually, the Light is all there *is* of you. But then he says that if the light that already is your Entirety seems to be darkness—ignorance—that darkness will appear to be very great indeed. Paraphrased, this last statement of Jesus may be read: "If the knowledge (Light) that you *are* could be ignorance (darkness, absence of Mind), how complete would that ignorance (absence of Mind) be."

Yes, total ignorance would be total darkness, or total absence of Mind. As you know, this would be impossible. You do not perceive dualistically. You do perceive as the single eye, *I*. You are the knowledge of the fact that *God really is All, All really is God*. Therefore, you are conscious of the Body of Light. But you are also aware of *being* the Mind—complete

Knowledge—that *is* this Body of ever-perfect, living Light.

Often during a class, a lecture, or an interview, someone will say, "Why, your whole Body is Light." Again, it often happens that during a class session many of those who are present will see not only this Body of Light, but they will also see every Body to be comprised of Light. Frequently the entire room will be a blaze of glorious, brilliant Light. Why does all of this take place? It happens because the students are aware of *being* the Mind that is full Knowledge. In short, they are aware of *being* the Light.

All Substance is intelligent because all Substance is the Mind that is Light and not darkness—ignorance. Life, Mind, Consciousness, Love are the substance of the Body of Light, and there is no other body. There is no body of darkness. There is no substance comprised of ignorance, absence of Mind, that can possibly exist as *any* body.

The Mind you are is steady, constant, and always equally present. The Mind you are does not change. The Mind you are is never more nor less. The Mind you are does not vacillate between knowing and not knowing.

The Consciousness you are is steady, constant, and always equally present. The Consciousness you are does not change. The Consciousness you are is never more nor less conscious. The Consciousness you are does not vacillate between being conscious and being unconsciousness.

The Life you are is steady, constant, and always equally present. The Life you are does not begin, nor can It end. The Life you are does not change. The Life you are is never more, nor is It ever any less alive. The Life you are does not vacillate between being alive and not being alive. *There is neither birth nor death.*

The Love you are is steady, constant, and always equally present. The Love you are does not change. The Love you are is never any more nor any less loving. The Love you are does not vacillate between being loving and being unloving.

And this, Beloved, is the Substance in Form that is your Body of Light.

Chapter XIX

All Illusion Is Mass Illusion

Once again, it is necessary to speak of the nothingness called illusion. You know, we cannot be dualistic even when we consider the nothingness we call illusion. There is no such thing — even in the seeming world of illusion — as division. No one can even *seem* to have a separate illusion. To most of us, it has appeared that any false sense of anything was our own separate illusion. (The nature of illusion is duality, twoness, or otherness.)

What we are saying here is paradoxical because we are speaking of nothing, and yet we are making it appear to be "something." But bear with us for a moment, and you will perceive just why we must speak in this way.

We are so accustomed to falsely believing that we are separate beings, with separate substances in forms called bodies, that it is not surprising that it would appear that we entertain separate illusions. Actually, it *seems* that we are inclined to claim some illusory misconception as our own separate or special illusion. What is to follow immediately should be most helpful in obliterating any false sense that you possess, or are possessed by, some illusion:

All that seems to be illusion is mass illusion.
Even this nothingness is not separated into separate
or divided illusions.

We have spoken much about the boundless,
indivisible ocean of living Light and the fact that this
Light is *one* indivisible, omniactive Substance. Well,
the fact is that the nothingness called illusion is also
boundless, omnipresent, omniactive, and indivisible. It
is as though a mass of ignorance were superimposed
upon the genuine universal Mind that is all Knowledge, and it seems that this superimposition of
ignorance—nothingness—conceals the glorious,
omnipresent Mind that *is*.

Now, we know that our *only* Identity is the one
inseparable, omnipresent, universal *I*. We also know
better than to even seem to identify ourselves with
or as an "I" that does not exist. But it does seem that the
fallacious, born individual identifies himself or herself
with the mass illusion, and this false identification
makes it appear that the individual possesses, or
is possessed by, an illusory mind, life, consciousness,
and body.

It is as though, at what is called birth, we surren-
dered our Identity and submitted to a false sense of
being a separate, temporary identity. In other words,
it seems that we become unaware of our genuine
and only indivisible Identity, and we began to
identify ourselves with a mass illusion which seems
to be duality itself. Of course, you realize that in this
apparent loss of identity, we seemed to identify

ourselves with darkness, ignorance, rather than with Light, or complete Knowledge. This mistaken sense of identity is why we have seemed to be so ignorant of what we genuinely are.

Now that we know what we genuinely are, we know what our genuine Identity is. We know that we are the universal Mind that is all Knowledge, and we know that as this Mind we are indivisible. Thus, never again will we even seem to misidentify ourselves with or as the nothingness of mass ignorance or absence of Mind. We are *not* a separate mind, and we do not claim to be a separate mind that is deluded as separated illusion.

Illusion is not Substance. It does not exist at all, so how can it exist in or as form? Illusion is not active. In order that there be activity, there would have to be substance to act. Again we say: *illusion is not substance; it is not form, and it cannot be active*. There is no illusory body, and there is no mind that knows itself to be, or to have, an illusory body. *Ignorance is not power because ignorance is not a presence; it is not present*. Never has there been a living, or alive, illusion. Never has there been a "nothingness" that was a presence or power. Never has there been an ignorant mind, nor has there been an unconscious consciousness.

You will find the entire basis for this revelation of so-called mass illusion in the chapter entitled "Identity" in our textbook, *The Ultimate*. Beloved, it will be most helpful if you will seriously study and contemplate this chapter on mass illusion.

Words of Importance

There are some vitally important words in our Ultimate vocabulary, and it is essential that we explore some of these words and their spiritual significance. We have already mentioned the words *Constancy* and *constant*. We have perceived some of the importance of these words and their meaning. But now let us go deeper into the great significance of these words.

Any word that is a statement of Principle Itself means more than does a word that could be considered an attribute of Principle. Thus, to speak the words *Constant* or *Constancy* with the perception that these words really symbolize a universal Truth, Fact, or Principle, is very meaningful.

To say, "I am constantly aware of this Truth" does not mean quite the same thing as does the statement, "I am the Constancy that *is* this Truth." In like manner, when we say, "I am a universal Constant," we have stated that we are the Principle — Constancy — or the universal Constant that is Constancy. This statement, perceived and uttered in full knowledge of its significance, is helpful, inspiring, and enlightening. It reveals the fact that we are the Principle — Constancy — that is an everlasting and uninterrupted Presence. It is this clear perception that enables us to perceive and to manifest a constant awareness of being what we are rather than to experience a fluctuating sense of enlightenment, often followed by apparent darkness.

There is quite an illusion, particularly among those of the Buddhist faith, that the Constancy that is eternal Life is interrupted over and over again by many births and many deaths. If this were true, it would mean that the eternal, constant Body was not constant. It would mean that the identity must acquire another body at each birth and that he must discard a body at death. The Constancy of all Substance in Form precludes the possibility of bodies that appear and disappear.

There may seem to be a fluctuation of our Supply. It may appear that it is always a feast or a famine. Perhaps today we are aware of an abundance of wealth, health, strength, etc., and next week, month, or next year, it may seem that any one—or all—of these normal evidences of Supply may be absent.

Right here is where the word *Constancy* is of great importance. Here is where we can say:

> I am the Constancy that is uninterrupted Supply, whether it be wealth, health, strength, or whatever.

Perhaps it may seem that you are joyous and free today and that tomorrow you are depressed and feel in bondage. Do you see how wonderfully helpful is the revelation that you are the Principle—Constancy—Itself? In this perception, you transcend all experiences that *seem* to fluctuate or to be interrupted. It would be well for you to frequently contemplate the fact that you are Constancy Itself.

You know, Indivisibility is a universal Principle. It is helpful to say, "I am indivisible." But it is more meaningful to say, "I am Indivisibility Itself." An important aspect of this word *Indivisibility* is that it also means *Love*. It is Love that makes our indivisible Oneness. It is well to realize that you are Love — the Principle Itself. It is good to know that you love, or that you are loving. But it means more to perceive that you are the universal, constant, inseparable Principle which is Love.

In like manner, it helps to perceive that you are perfect. But to realize that you are Perfection Itself has a far greater and more powerful significance. To say that you are eternal is to speak well and truly. But to say, "I am Eternality Itself" means to make a statement that is fraught with power.

This is why Jesus said, "I am life. I am truth. I am the way." He was stating the great fact that he was the universal, constant, eternal Principle which is Life, Truth, and the Way. Oh, "the Way," rightly understood, is a universal Principle. The Way is the Absolute Truth, and the Absolute Truth is certainly a universal, constant Principle.

Of course, it is not necessary now to mention the fact that you, of yourself or by yourself, as a separate identity, can do nothing, know nothing, have nothing, and be nothing. But now you know that because you *are* the eternal, complete, universal All, or I AM, you can and do know All because you are *The All*. Now you can perceive clearly, and all the way, the indivisible, invincible, eternal, immutable Perfection that you are. And in great Joy, Humility, and complete Awareness, you can say, "I AM THAT I AM."

I am eternal Life, everlastingly alive. *I* am eternal Consciousness, eternally conscious. *I* am eternal Mind, forever knowing all that *I* am. *I* am eternal Love, everlastingly aware of being the indivisible, inseparable Love—Oneness—that *I* am.

I am Eternality Itself. *I* am Constancy. *I* am the uninterrupted Constancy that never fluctuates. *I* am eternally, constantly perfect, for *I* am Perfection. *I* am everlastingly alive, for *I* am eternal, constant Life. *I* am the complete aggregate—sum total—of all Truth. *I* am Completeness. *I* am Truth. *I* am the sum total of every Truth that constitutes the whole, the sum total, the totality, the All.

I know every Truth that *I* am. *I* am every Truth that *I* know. *I* am omniscient, for *I* am Omniscience. Thus, *I* am all Knowledge. *I* am the Mind that knows all Truth. *I* am the Truth that is all Knowledge.

All of this *I* am, for I AM THAT I AM.

About the Author

During early childhood, Marie S. Watts began questioning: "Why am I? What am I? Where is God? What is God?"

After experiencing her first illumination at seven years of age, her hunger for the answers to these questions became intensified. Although she became a concert pianist, her search for the answers continued, leading her to study all religions, including those of the East.

Finally, ill and unsatisfied, she gave up her profession of music, discarded all books of ancient and modern religions, kept only the Bible, and went into virtual seclusion from the world for some eight years. It was out of the revelations and illuminations she experienced during those years, revelations that were sometimes the very opposite of what she had hitherto believed, that her own healing was realized.

During all the previous years, she had been active in helping others. After 1957, she devoted herself exclusively to the continuance of this healing work and to lecturing and teaching. Revelations continually came to her, and these have been set forth in this and every book.

To all seekers for Truth, for God, for an understanding of their own true Being, the words in her books will speak to your soul.

Made in the USA
Charleston, SC
03 December 2016